Caribbean Primary Mathematics

Level 6

Delia Samuel-Cenac

Together with: June Playfair, Ernie Johnson, Agatha James and Sheyla Constantine, Yvette James-Brown, Joanna Redhead, Dr Sandra Trotman, Sonia Severin, Benita Byer, Joseph Serieux, Jeffrey Blaize, Simon Sharplis, Hyacinth S Dorleon, Twain Edward, Elaine Lewis, Lydon Richardson, Wendy Griffith, Patterson Abraham.

Ginn

Contents

Introduction

Caribbean Primary Mathematics offers a spiral approach to learning, where concepts are introduced, explained, practised and reinforced at regular intervals. This ensures that each child can continuously build on and clarify his or her understanding of the basic mathematical concepts.

At Level 6 the Pupil Book is a colourful write-in workbook that provides a refreshing and enjoyable guide to the world of numeracy. There is also an accompanying Teacher's Guide, as well as a Practice Workbook that provides extra questions on topics covers in the Pupil Book.

On the inside back cover of the Level 6 Pupil Book you will find a **new CD-ROM** containing ten interactive games. The CD-ROM is designed to be easy to use and provides opportunities for pupils to reinforce their learning in a fun and interactive way. The symbol in the Teacher's Guide indicates where there is opportunity on the CD-ROM for further practise of a particular skill or topic covered in the Pupil Book.

How to install and use the CD-ROM
This product is suitable for use on PCs. If the CD-ROM is loaded into a CD drive on a PC it should autorun. If it does not, please go to My Computer (Computer on Vista), click on the CD drive, and double click on RB31.exe.

Minimum system requirements
PC
Windows 2000 or XP Pro or Vista
Internet Explorer 6 (or higher) or Firefox 2.0 (or higher)
Flash Player 8 (or higher) plug-in
Software that is capable of opening .doc (Microsoft Office Word) – Microsoft Office 2000 recommended
Adobe ® Reader ® 7

Hardware
Pentium III 900 MHZ with 256Mb RAM

Working with numbers

This chapter examines ways of counting, reading and writing numbers. It also deals with some operations on numbers. There are many ways of writing numbers. Rounding off to the nearest ten or hundred helps us to work with large numbers – tens and hundreds of thousands, millions and even billions. Another way we can express large numbers is by using exponents of 10. The exponent is the small raised number that tells us the power to which the number must be raised – the number of times the number must be multiplied by itself. For example, $10^4 = 10 \times 10 \times 10 \times 10$. This is another way of writing 10 000 or 10 to the power of 4.

Counting

People count in many different ways. Sometimes you may need to count on from 0 or a given number, at other times you may need to count backwards from a given number. You can start counting at any given number and you can count in ones (1, 2, 3 …) or you can skip count by counting in different groups of numbers (10, 15, 20 …).

The photo shows a crowd of people watching a cricket match. Can you tell how many people are in the crowd? How could you use the photo to work out approximately how many people attended this cricket match?

A   Identify the counting pattern in each number line. Copy and complete each pattern.

1   1 000 1 200 1 400

2   1 750 1 500 1 250

B   Copy the counting patterns and write the next four numbers in each.

1.   24, 28, 32, ____, ____, ____, ____

2.   150, 350, 550, ____, ____, ____, ____

3.   2 500, 2 250, 2 000, ____, ____, ____, ____

Farmer Brown says he has 25 000 banana plants on his farm. List at least five methods he could have used to count or work out how many plants he has.

Large numbers in figures and words

A   The table shows how many slabs of chocolate were sold by eight supermarkets during one month.

Supermarkets	Number of slabs sold
Appleton Store	1 460 305
Brown's Bargains	30 700
Chain Store	9 407 518
Dennis & Co	300 924
Everything Shop	8 946 503
Fresh Food Store	600 001
Grocery Garden	16 305
Hunter & Son	6 000 001

1.   Which supermarket made sales of six hundred thousand and one slabs?

2.   Which supermarket made the most sales?

3.   Write in words how many slabs were sold by:
   a   Dennis & Co
   b   Everything Shop
   c   Grocery Garden
   d   Hunter & Son

B   1   These are the numbers of boxes of bananas and boxes of oranges sent to four countries. Copy the table, writing figures instead of words.

Countries	Boxes of bananas	Boxes of oranges
Canada	three million, five hundred thousand and fifty	three million and nine
United Kingdom	two million, seven hundred and sixty thousand, three hundred and twenty-five	nine hundred and twenty-seven thousand, six hundred and fifty
United States of America	four million, five hundred and eighty	one and a half million
Germany	three-quarters of a million	one and a quarter million

2 Copy the table and write the value of the underlined digit in the space provided. The first one has been done for you.

Number	Value of digit
4 1<u>5</u>6	5 tens = 50
1<u>5</u>2 309	
1 <u>8</u>00 007	
2 419 0<u>2</u>4	
852 <u>6</u>00	
3 93<u>6</u>	

Using powers of 10

$10^0 = 1$ $10^1 = 10$ $10^2 = 100$ $10^3 = 1\,000$

$24\,386 = (2 \times 10^4) + (4 \times 10^3) + (3 \times 10^2) + (8 \times 10^1) + (6 \times 10^0)$
$= (2 \times 10\,000) + (4 \times 1\,000) + (3 \times 100) + (8 \times 10) + (6 \times 1)$
$= 20\,000 + 4\,000 + 300 + 80 + 6$

This is called expanded notation, because we expand what each number represents.

A

1 Use powers to show the expanded notation for these numbers.
a   785
b   1 903
c   75 612
d   150 456
e   235 789
f   1 800 800

2 Write the expanded notation for these numbers.
a   158
b   425
c   5 674
d   99 234
e   145 335
f   9 655 159

3 What numbers are represented by:
a $(2 \times 10^6) + (3 \times 10^5) + (4 \times 10^2) + (4 \times 10^1) + (3 \times 10^0)$
b $(7 \times 10^5) + (2 \times 10^4) + (3 \times 10^3) + (2 \times 10^0)$
c $(2 \times 10^6) + (4 \times 10^2) + (1 \times 10^0)$
d $(4 \times 10^0) + (7 \times 10^5) + (4 \times 10^3) + (7 \times 10^2)$

Where do we use large numbers in real life? What is the largest number you have heard of or used?

Large numbers in real life

$120 944.00 — Mr John
$96 780.00 — Mr Binks
$49 440.00 — Ms Byer
$8 100.00 — Ms Brown
$4 800.00 — Ms Smith

A **1** Who earns the highest salary?

2 Who earns the lowest salary?

3 Write the salaries in order, starting with the lowest.

Country	Population
Norway	4 247 546
Barbuda	1 400
Barbados	269 000
Mauritius	1 180 000
Belize	242 000
Kuwait	1 970 000
Swaziland	984 000

B **1** The table shows some small countries. Which has the largest population?

2 Which country has a population of almost 1 million people?

3 Which countries have populations of more than 1 million people?

4 Which countries have populations of fewer than half a million people?

5 Write the populations of these countries in words:
    a Norway   b Barbuda   c Barbados

6 Write the populations of these countries in expanded notation:
    a Kuwait   b Swaziland

Comparing and ordering numbers

A Write each set of numbers in ascending order.

1 32 956, 437 694, 4 364, 438 943

2 943 624, 963 458, 936 438, 974 893

3 4 884 396, 4 483 630, 4 983 363, 4 889 363

B Write each set of numbers in descending order.

1. 67 384, 93 247, 1 482, 132 678

2. 78 943, 146 849, 94 361, 148 493

3. 3 468 952, 3 489 526, 3 474 361, 3 487 216

C Study the map and read the information carefully. You will need to use the information to answer the questions which follow.

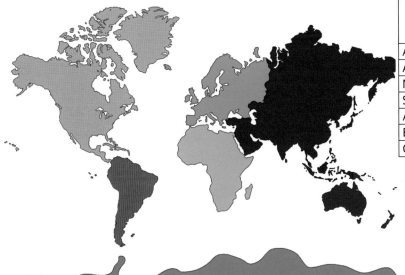

Continent	Area (km²)	Approx. population (in 2008)	
Asia	43,810,000	3,879,000,000	
Africa	30,370,000	922,011,000	
North America	24,490,000	528,720,588	
South America	17,840,000	382,000,000	
Antarctica	13,720,000	1,000	
Europe	10,180,000	731,000,000	
Oceania	8,500,000	32,000,000	

1. List the area (in km²) covered by each continent in ascending order.

2. List the population of each continent in order from greatest number of people to least number of people.

3. Name the continents that have an area greater than 25 million km².

4. List the continents with a population of less than half a billion.

5. Complete these sentences:
   a. The surface area of Europe is almost thrice the area of ____.
   b. There are more people living on ____ than on any other continent.
   c. There are fewer people living on ____ America than on ____ America.

Rounding off

To round off a number to the nearest power of 10, examine the digit in the relevant place (e.g. to round off to the nearest 100, look at the digit in the hundreds place). Add 1 to this digit if the digit to its right is 5 or more. Then replace the digits to its right with zeros.
For example: round off 52 913 to the nearest 1 000.
Add 1 to 2 since 9 is greater than 5. The answer is 53 000.
52 913 to the nearest 10 is 52 910.
52 913 to the nearest 100 is 52 900.

A **1** Round off to the nearest 10.

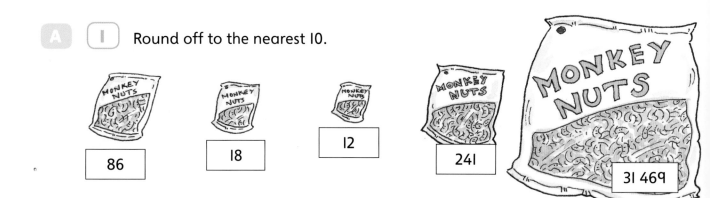

86   18   12   241   31 469

2 Round off to the nearest 100.

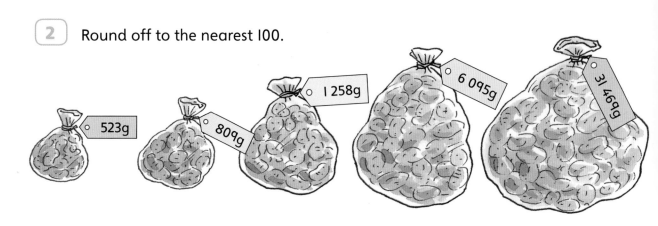

523g   809g   1 258g   6 095g   31 469g

3 a Round off to the nearest 1 000.

$8 632 $2 745 $9 034 $12 634 $10 999

b Arrange the prices in descending order.

B Write these in figures, then round off each number to the nearest thousand.
a seven hundred and nine thousand, eight hundred and seventy-five
b seventeen thousand, six hundred and twenty-three
c sixty-seven thousand, two hundred and seven
d quarter of a million

C These are the highest mountains on each continent. Round each height off to the nearest 1 metre, the nearest 10 metres and the nearest 100 metres. Find out the heights of ten other mountains, and make a chart showing their heights.

Continent	Mountain	Height (m)	To nearest 1m	To nearest 10m	To nearest 100m
South America	Aconcagua	6 959			
Africa	Kilimanjaro	5 895			
Antarctica	Vinson Massif	4 897			
Australia	Kosciusko	2 228			
Asia	Everest	8 848			
Europe	Elbrus	5 642			
North America	McKinley	6 194			

Different number systems

The numbers we use today are called Hindu-Arabic numerals. The Romans used a different way of writing numbers. They used letters.

I = 1   V = 5   X = 10   L = 50   C = 100   M = 1 000

Hindu-Arabic	1	2	3	4	5	6	7	8	9	10
Roman	I	II	III	IV	V	VI	VII	VIII	IX	X

Hindu-Arabic	10	20	30	40	50	60	70	80	90	100
Roman	X	XX	XXX	XL	L	LX	LXX	LXXX	XC	C

A

1 Describe how the Roman numeral system differs from ours.

2 Write the values of these Roman numerals in Hindu-Arabic numerals.
  a XV   b LIV   c CM   d MMCXX

3 Write the value of these Hindu-Arabic numerals in Roman numerals.
  a 7   b 89   c 140   d 8 275

B Try to write the following in Roman numerals.
  a your phone number   b your birth date   c the current year

The Romans wrote by carving into tablets of stone. What difficulties do you think they encountered with this method of writing? Do you think it would be easy or difficult to use the Roman numeral system today? Why? Think about the kinds of numbers we use every day: phone numbers, reference numbers, ID numbers and passwords on computers.

Chapter 2

Number theory

This chapter examines types of numbers such as odd, even, prime, composite and square numbers. It also deals with factors, multiples and number sequencing. Understanding how numbers work helps us to work quickly to check our calculations. Some numbers have special properties. Even numbers are multiples of 2, which means they can be divided by 2. This also means that 2 is a factor of all even numbers. Odd numbers can't be divided by 2. Prime numbers can only be divided by themselves, and by 1. When a number is multiplied by itself (as in 8×8), the result is a square number, and the original number is its square root.

Review of odd, even, prime and composite numbers

A   Copy and complete this table by putting a ✔ in the correct columns.

Number	Odd	Even	Prime	Composite
24		✔		✔
38				
83				
15				
21				
17				
64				
91				
82				

B

1   Find the products, and use your solutions to help you complete the rule.
   a $4 \times 6 =$ b $2 \times 10 =$ c $4 \times 8 =$ d $6 \times 8 =$ e $10 \times 6 =$
   Even number × even number = _____ number.

2   Find the products, and use your solutions to help you complete the rule.
   a $7 \times 3 =$ b $1 \times 5 =$ c $9 \times 5 =$ d $3 \times 11 =$ e $13 \times 7 =$
   Odd number × odd number = _____ number.

3   Make up five multiplication sums to help you prove and complete this rule.
   Odd number × even number = _____ number.

C

1   Write each set of numbers.
   a   Odd numbers less than 20   b   Even numbers less than 20
   c   Prime numbers less than 20   d   Composite numbers less than 20

2   a   Only one even number is prime. Which one is it?
   b   Is 1 a prime number? Give reasons for your answer.
   c   What is the largest number you can make from the digits 8, 6, 9, 1? Explain how you made the number.

Factors, prime factorisation and the highest common factor

A factor of a given number is a number that divides into the given number and leaves no remainder.
For example: factors of 6 are 1, 2, 3 and 6.

A **1** Write all the factors of these numbers.
   a   42   b   38   c   30   d   90   e   100

A prime number is a number whose only factors are 1 and itself. A prime factor is a factor that is a prime number.
For example: 7 is a prime number. Prime factors of 6 are 2 and 3.

2 Write all the factors of 12 and of 45. Circle the prime factors.

3 Copy and complete this table.

Numbers	Factors	Prime factors
16	1, 2, 4, 8, 16	2
20		
30		
18		
65		

The highest common factor (HCF) of a set of numbers is a number that divides into each of the numbers in the set without leaving a remainder.

B **1** The HCF of 6 and 15 is 3. The HCF of 14 and 21 is 7. Can you explain why?

2 Find the HCF of each set.
   a   20 and 24   b   36 and 27   c   12, 18 and 30

3 a   What is the largest number that divides into 42 and 48 without leaving a remainder?
   b   What is the largest number that divides into 26 and 37 leaving a remainder of 4 in each case?

These are factor trees. The main branches show the factors of the number in the trunk. The smaller branches show the factors of the numbers in the main branches. We can express a number as the products of its prime factors. This is called prime factorisation.

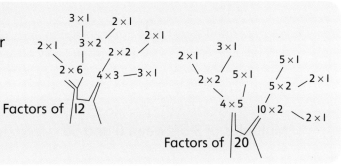

C Draw a factor tree for each number and express it as a product of its prime factors.
   a   24   b   18   c   28   d   36   e   50

Multiples and the lowest common multiple

The multiples of a number x are numbers which are exactly divisible by x.
For example: multiples of 2 are: 2, 4, 6, 8, 10, 12, 14, 16, 18, 20, ...

The common multiple of a set of numbers is a multiple shared by all of the numbers.
For example: 10 and 20 are common multiples of 2 and 5.
12 is a common multiple of 2, 3, 4 and 6.

The lowest common multiple (LCM) of a set of numbers is the smallest number that is exactly divisible by each number in the set.
For example: The multiples of 2 are: 2, 4, 6, 8, 10, ...
The multiples of 3 are: 3, 6, 9, 12, 15, ...
The LCM of 2 and 3 is 6. This is the lowest multiple common to both numbers.

A **1** Multiples of 8 are: 8, 16, 24, 32, 40, 48, ...
Multiples of 12 are: 12, 24, 36, 48, ...
The LCM of 8 and 12 is 24. Why?

2 In the same way, find the LCM of these sets of numbers.
a 5 and 6   b 2, 3 and 4

B **1** a Copy the diagram. Fill in the multiples of each of the circled sets.
b Fill in the common multiples in the overlapping area between the sets.
c Underline the lowest common multiple.

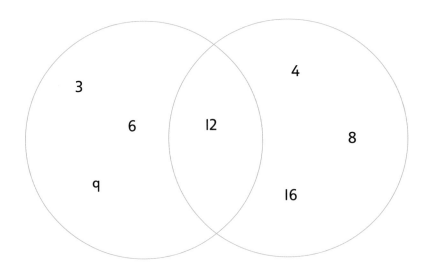

Multiples of 3 between 0 and 50   Multiples of 4 between 0 and 50

Finding the LCM using prime factorisation

Find the LCM of 12 and 18 using prime factorisation.
First write each number as a product of its prime factors.
12 = <u>2 × 2</u> × 3
18 = 2 × <u>3 × 3</u>
Next, take the biggest group for each prime factor and write it down.
2 × 2 × 3 × 3
∴ LCM of 12 and 18 = 36

A **1** Find the LCM using prime factorisation.
- a 25 and 30
- b 12 and 14
- c 4, 6 and 8
- d 5, 7 and 8
- e 7, 9 and 12
- f 15, 20 and 24

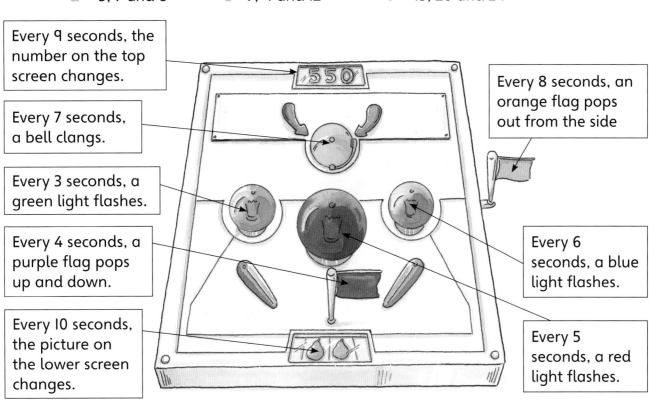

Every 9 seconds, the number on the top screen changes.

Every 7 seconds, a bell clangs.

Every 3 seconds, a green light flashes.

Every 4 seconds, a purple flag pops up and down.

Every 10 seconds, the picture on the lower screen changes.

Every 8 seconds, an orange flag pops out from the side

Every 6 seconds, a blue light flashes.

Every 5 seconds, a red light flashes.

B A scientist has built a machine with screens, lights, bells and flags. Using prime factorisation, work out the problems below.
- a After how many seconds will all three lights flash at the same time?
- b After how many seconds will the number screen and the picture screen change at the same time?
- c After how many seconds will both the flags pop out at the same time?
- d After how many seconds will the green light flash at the same time as the bell goes?
- e After how many seconds will the number on the top screen change at the same time as the orange flag pops out?
- f Make up two more questions about the machine's timing, and get your friend to answer them.

Assessment

A

1 The lollipops at Anna's shop are sold in strips of 6. What are the ten smallest numbers of lollipops you can buy from Anna's shop?

2 An automatic teller machine only gives money in multiples of $10. What are the ten smallest amounts a customer can withdraw from the machine?

3 Joan wants to buy at least 100 marbles. But the marbles are sold in bags of 8.
  a How many bags must she buy to get at least 100 marbles?
  b How many marbles will she have to buy altogether?

B

1 Write the following numbers as products of their prime factors.
  a 18   b 48   c 100

2 Write the next three multiples in each set.
  a {7, 14, ...}   b {11, 22, 33, ...}   c {6, 12, 18, ...}

C HCF game

You need: Small coins or counters, some paper and a pen.

How to play: You can play with 2, 3 or 4 people. The first player puts the counter onto the number grid so that the counter is touching two squares. Everyone tries to work out the HCF of the two numbers in the squares. The first person to work it out gets a point, and gets to throw the counter next. Decide how many points you need to win (for example, 10 or 25 points) and the first person to get that many points is the winner.

11	12	13	14	15
6	7	8	9	10
1	2	3	4	5
15	14	13	12	11
6	7	8	9	10

Square numbers and square roots

$3^2 = 3 \times 3 = 9$

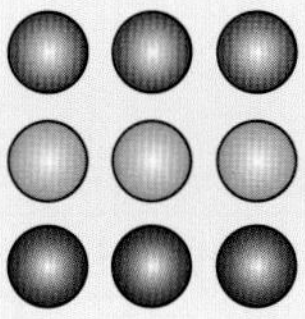

9 is a square number.
The square root of 9 is 3.
$\sqrt{9} = 3$
$\sqrt{}$ means square root.

1^2 2^2 3^2 4^2

A Do your own dot drawings to illustrate 5^2, 7^2, 8^2 and 10^2.

B Copy and complete the crossword puzzle using the clues in the box below. Write all the answers in words, not numerals.

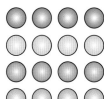

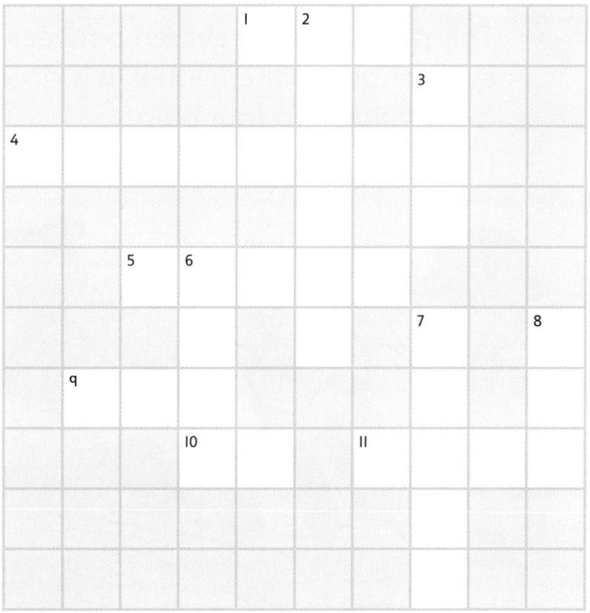

Across	Down
1 The square root of 100	2 The HCF of 22 and 55
4 The LCM of 2 and 7	3 1^2
5 The HCF of 49 and 35	6 Multiples of two are also called _____ numbers
9 A cube with the first six numbers on it is also called this	7 51 is the (first, third or fifth) multiple of 17?
10 Can a prime number have more than two factors?	8 The common factor of all prime numbers
11 The square root of 81	

Number sequences

A sequence is a list of numbers that follow a pattern. Try to describe these patterns.

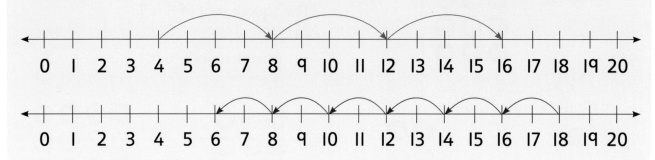

A   Copy and complete these sequences. You may use a calculator to help you. For each sequence, explain the pattern.

a   5, 9, 13, 17, ____, ____, ____

b   29, 27, 25, ____, ____, ____

c   4, 12, 36, ____, ____, ____

d   3 125, 625, 125, ____, ____, ____

e   5, 15, 45, ____, ____, ____

f   2, 5, 11, 23, ____, ____, ____

B   This pizza must be shared between a crowd of friends. When the pizza is cut straight across the middle, it is divided into two pieces. When it is cut a second time, it is divided into four pieces.

1   Copy and complete the table.

Number of cuts	1	2	3	4	5	6	7	8
Pieces of pizza	2	4						

2   a   What is the pattern in the first sequence (number of cuts)?

     b   What is the pattern in the second sequence (pieces of pizza)?

3   a   How many times would you cut the pizza to have enough pieces for everyone in your classroom?

     b   How big or small do you think the slices would be? Why?

Number theory

Number operations

We use numbers in different ways every day. In this chapter we will add, subtract, multiply and divide numbers to solve different problems.

A Many mathematical words are also used in daily life. Write each word with the definition that could fit that word.

Word	Definition
operation sum product addition of divide multiply solve	• have children • times one number by another • find a solution for a riddle or puzzle • a new person or object to join a group • a word used for percentages and fractions • a mathematical procedure involving +, − , x or ÷ • keep people or things apart • the total when you add numbers together • find a solution to a mathematical problem • a medical procedure that takes place in a hospital • an item made in a factory

Addition and subtraction facts

A How well do you remember your basic addition and subtraction facts? Try to do these exercises mentally, writing the answers only.

 1 Add.

a	83 + 3 =	830 + 30 =	83 000 + 30 =
b	49 + 6 =	490 + 60 =	49 000 + 60 =
c	78 + 8 =	780 + 80 =	78 000 + 80 =
d	83 + 30 =	8 300 + 30 =	83 000 + 300 =
e	49 + 60 =	4 900 + 60 =	49 000 + 600 =
f	78 + 80 =	7 800 + 80 =	78 000 + 800 =
g	830 + 3 =	83 000 + 3 =	83 000 + 3 000 =
h	490 + 6 =	49 000 + 6 =	49 000 + 6 000 =
i	780 + 8 =	78 000 + 8 =	78 000 + 8 000 =

2 Subtract.

a	43 − 6 =	430 − 60 =	4 300 − 60 =	43 000 − 60 =
b	94 − 7 =	940 − 70 =	9 400 − 70 =	94 000 − 70 =
c	71 − 8 =	710 − 80 =	7 100 − 80 =	71 000 − 80 =
d	430 − 6 =	4 300 − 6 =	43 000 − 6 =	43 000 − 600 =
e	940 − 7 =	9 400 − 7 =	94 000 − 7 =	94 000 − 700 =
f	710 − 8 =	7 100 − 8 =	71 000 − 8 =	71 000 − 800 =

3 These addition sums are all incorrect. Rewrite the sums with the correct answers.

a 36 + 66 = 100   b   28 + 82 = 100
c 53 + 57 = 100   d   49 + 61 = 100
e 33 + 66 = 100   f   11 + 79 = 100
g 73 + 37 = 100   h   45 + 54 = 100
i 85 + 25 = 100   j   9 + 90 = 100

4 Find the missing digits in these subtractions.

a 264 − 99 = 1____   b   362 − 199 = 1____   c   488 − 199 = 2____
d 344 − 199 = 1____   e   428 − 198 = 2____   f   365 − 199 = ____

C Can you solve this coding problem?

Each digit from 1 to 9 is represented by a different letter from a to i. Zero is not written in code, so 0 represents zero. Study the sums carefully and work out which letters are used to represent each digit.

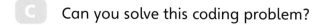

| g00 + g00 = a000 | hg0 + hg0 = g00 | ig0 + ig0 = f00 | eg0 + eg0 = d00 |

| bi0 + if0 = a000 | eg0 + gg0 = a000 | hc0 + fh0 = a000 | ad0 + ca0 = a000 |

D **1** Do the following addition sums.

a   23   b   52   c   75   d   18   e   39   f   56
     + 36   + 34   + 22   + 13   + 12   + 17

2 Find the sum.

a 142 + 117 + 131 =   b   270 + 2 114 + 1 309 =
c 265 + 173 + 391 + 995 =   d   1 494 + 5 282 + 8 123 =
e 547 + 80 + 608 + 8 875 + 2 137 =   f   356 + 802 + 495 + 1 248 + 9 667 =

3 The table shows the number of minutes Roy spent in training over five days. For how many minutes did Roy train altogether?

Day of the week	Time spent training in minutes
Monday	140
Tuesday	145
Wednesday	125
Thursday	150
Friday	175

More operations

Continent	Area (km²)
Asia	31 880 000
Africa	30 312 000
North America	21 776 000
South America	20 546 000
Antarctica	13 300 000
Europe	23 049 000
Australia	8 564 000

A

1 a Which is the largest continent?
  b Which is the smallest continent?

2 a How much larger is Africa than North America?
  b How much larger is Asia than Europe?
  c How much larger is South America than Australia?

3 a What is the combined land area of Europe and Asia?
  b What is the combined land area of North America and South America?

B Play this game with a friend, taking turns. Copy the numbers in the ring. Circle any two numbers, and find their sum (add them together). Choose the correct box from below to 'post' your answer into. If your choice is correct, you get the number of points on the box.
Continue circling pairs of numbers until all the numbers are circled. You may not circle a number more than once.

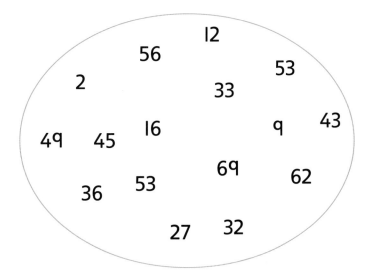

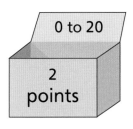
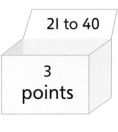

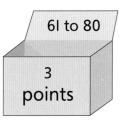
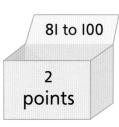

0 to 20 — 2 points
21 to 40 — 3 points
41 to 60 — 4 points
61 to 80 — 3 points
81 to 100 — 2 points

Subtraction

Important terms for subtraction
minus   take away   find the difference   how much less?   how many fewer?

Computer games
Six friends took turns playing computer games. At the end of the game, each player gets their penalties deducted from their points.

Mark · 1 691 points — 550 penalties
Angela · 5 248 points — 1 205 penalties
Lucille · 92 100 points — 1 000 penalties
Nicky · 85 768 points — 2 437 penalties
Dina · 99 765 points — 5 415 penalties
Bob · 77 844 points — 620 penalties

A **1** Deduct the penalties from the points to work out each of the children's total scores. Write the totals in a table like the one below.

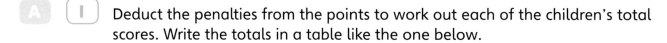

Names	Mark	Angela	Lucille	Nicky	Dina	Bob
Total scores						

2
a Write the penalties in ascending order (from lowest to highest).
b Write the points in descending order (from highest to lowest).
c Write the total scores in ascending order.

3
a Between which two children is there the greatest difference in scores? Explain how you know this.

4
a Work out the difference between Angela's score and Mark's score.
b Work out the difference between Lucille's score and Nicky's score.
c Work out the difference between Dina's score and Bob's score.

5
a Work out the difference between Angela's penalties and Mark's penalties.
b Work out the difference between Lucille's penalties and Nicky's penalties.
c Work out the difference between Dina's penalties and Bob's penalties.

B **1** Find the answers.
a 4 798 – 1 306 =
b 5 014 – 3 973 =
c 5 432 – 2 119 =
d 1 754 – 235 =
e 8 970 – 401 =
f 3 375 – 290 =

2 Subtract.
a 11 835 – 10 284 =
b 751 815 – 622 294 =
c 99 000 – 95 =
d 457 800 – 329 474 =
e 121 625 – 115 226 =
f 88 930 – 4 785

More subtraction

In these magic squares, all the lines of numbers (across, down and diagonally) add up to the same total.

a   Copy and complete the magic squares.

b   In pairs, make up two magic squares of your own, using numbers greater than 5 000. You can use a calculator.

c   Copy your magic squares, leaving four of the numbers missing, and exchange them with another pair. See who can work them out the fastest.

4	3	8
	5	1
	7	6

16		12
	15	19
		14

		212
213	215	217
218		

B

a

22 Smith Avenue
$77 889

b

152 Long Street
$192 559

c

5 Palm Road
$272 995

a

15 Factory Road
$65 779

b

96 High Street
$95 999

c

85 Millionaire's Row
$895 999

1   Work out the difference in price between each pair of houses.
  a   22 Smith Avenue and 15 Factory Road
  b   96 High Street and 152 Long Street
  c   5 Palm Road and 85 Millionaires' Row

2   Write the prices in ascending order.

3   a   Between which two houses is there the greatest difference in price?
    b   Work out the difference in price between those two houses.

4 The prices on the previous page do not include tax. The table on the right shows what four buyers paid in total for their houses, including tax. Work out how much tax was added onto each price.

House	Amount paid
96 High Street	$107 520
15 Factory Road	$73 675
152 Long Street	$219 517
85 Millionaire's Row	$1 021 438

5 The house at 5 Palm Road was sold for less than the advertised price. The seller accepted a price of $255 875. How much less did she receive than the advertised price?

Multiplication and division facts

A How well do you remember your basic multiplication and division facts? Try to do these exercises mentally, writing the answers only.

1 Try to finish these multiplications in 2 minutes.

a $3 \times 5 =$ _____ b $4 \times 8 =$ _____ c $4 \times 9 =$ _____ d $6 \times 9 =$ _____

e $6 \times 2 =$ _____ f $6 \times 8 =$ _____ g $5 \times 8 =$ _____ h $10 \times 3 =$ _____

i $9 \times 2 =$ _____ j $5 \times 5 =$ _____ k $7 \times 7 =$ _____ l $9 \times 7 =$ _____

m $10 \times 5 =$ _____ n $7 \times 1 =$ _____ o $6 \times 10 =$ _____ p $8 \times 8 =$ _____

q $7 \times 3 =$ _____ r $5 \times 9 =$ _____ s $8 \times 9 =$ _____ t $3 \times 9 =$ _____

2 Fill in the missing numbers in each pair of problems.

a _____ $\times 5 = 45$ $45 \div 5 =$ _____

b _____ $\times 7 = 21$ $21 \div 7 =$ _____

c _____ $\times 8 = 16$ $16 \div 8 =$ _____

d _____ $\times 6 = 30$ $30 \div 6 =$ _____

e $4 \times 4 =$ _____   _____ $\div 4 = 4$

f _____ $\times 3 = 24$ $24 \div 3 =$ _____

g _____ $\times 4 = 28$ $28 \div 4 =$ _____

h _____ $\times 6 = 54$ $54 \div 6 =$ _____

i _____ $\times 7 = 56$ $56 \div 7 =$ _____

3 Without doing any division, say which numbers in each set will divide exactly by 2.

a 35   64   53   88   92

b 36   49   60   81   32

c 109   346   943   806   778

d 708   140   200   388   279

4 The following divisions are all incorrect. Rewrite them with the correct answers.

a $42 \div 6 = 8$ b $66 \div 6 = 12$ c $72 \div 9 = 9$

d $35 \div 7 = 6$ e $96 \div 4 = 22$ f $87 \div 3 = 22$

Multiplication

A   Choose and write down the words or phrases associated with multiplication.

find the product	take away	times	multiply	find the sum
squared	to the power of	find the difference		exponent

When you multiply whole numbers by 10 or powers of 10, you get zeros in your answers. Any whole number multiplied by 10 gets one zero. If it is multiplied by 100 it gets two zeroes, and so on.

$15 \times 10 = 150$ (one zero)

$15 \times 100 = 1\ 500$ $15 \times 1\ 000 = 15\ 000$ $15 \times 10\ 000 = 150\ 000$

B   **1**   Write these numbers both as powers of ten, and in words. For example:
$1\ 000 = 10^3 =$ one thousand
    a   10   b   10 000   c   1 000 000   d   100 000   e   1

     2   Write these numbers in expanded notation, showing the multiples of 10. For example:
$5\ 672 = (5 \times 1\ 000) + (6 \times 100) + (7 \times 10) + (2 \times 1)$
$ = (5 \times 10^3) + (6 \times 10^2) + (7 \times 10^1) + (2 \times 10^0)$

    a   7 849   b   27 451   c   90 528   d   659 203   e   5 300 706

     3   Cutting Edge is a clothes manufacturing business. It uses 4 metres of cloth to make a suit. It uses 2 metres of cloth to make men's trousers, and 2 metres of cloth to make ladies' trousers. It uses 1 metre of cloth to make a scarf.
How much cloth is needed for:
    a   100 suits
    b   10 suits
    c   100 men's trousers
    d   1 000 ladies' trousers
    e   1 000 scarves

C   **1**   Find the product.
    a $351 \times 90 =$ b $185 \times 20 =$ c $4\ 271 \times 30 =$
    d $9\ 006 \times 80 =$ e $8\ 050 \times 30 =$ f $3\ 461 \times 60 =$

     2   Find the product.
    a $73 \times 21 =$ b $40 \times 37 =$ c $68 \times 26 =$
    d $65 \times 83 =$ e $418 \times 86 =$ f $297 \times 62 =$

More multiplication

The Sprinters running club arranged a fun run to raise money for charity. The first sponsor, Sitting Duck Office Equipment, agreed to pay $2 for each kilometre run by each runner. The second sponsor, Mr Chang Chinese Restaurant, agreed to pay $3 for each kilometre run by each runner. Here are the distances covered by the top five runners:

Name	Distance in km
Dennis Soba	72
Angela Pick	70
Rita Pringle	69
Lizzy Pringle	68
Sam Lee	65

1. Work out how much each sponsor paid for each of the five runners.

2. Dennis took 2 minutes per kilometre. How long did he take to run his race?

3. Angela took 3 minutes per kilometre. How long did she take to run her race?

4. Sam took twice as long as Dennis. How long did he take to run her race?

5. Megan ran 17 km. Tina ran three times as far as Megan. How far did Tina run?

B

Ms Morris's suitcase contains three items, each weighing 6 kg.
Mr Mack's bag weighs twice as much as Ms Morris' suitcase.
Miss Smith's bag contains two items of 5 kg each, and three items of 3 kg each.
Mr Briggs' luggage weighs twice as much as Miss Smith's.
Work out the weight of each passenger's piece of luggage.

C

School A has 175 students. School B has 4 more students than school A. School C has 4 times as many students as school A. What is the total number of students in the three schools?

Division

1 Write the answers only.

a 413 000 ÷ 10 = _____

b 413 000 ÷ 100 = _____

c 413 000 ÷ 1 000 = _____

2 Write the answers only.

a 64 000 ÷ _____ = 64

b 64 000 ÷ _____ = 640

c 64 000 ÷ _____ = 6 400

3 Write definitions for each of these words. Use a dictionary if you need one, and use this example to explain your definition: 18 ÷ 3 = 6.

a quotient

b divisor

c factor

d multiple

e remainder

Look at these examples carefully.

4 104 ÷ 9 =

```
                  quotient
          456
divisor 9)4 104   dividend
          36
          50
          45
          54
          54
           0
```

1 568 ÷ 13 =

```
                  quotient
          120  rem 8  remainder
divisor 13)1 568
           13         dividend
           26
           26
           08
           00
            8
```

B

1 Work these out.

a 800 ÷ 5

b 906 ÷ 6

c 840 ÷ 7

d 9 000 ÷ 8

e 8 007 ÷ 5

f 5 432 ÷ 8

2 Find the quotient using long division.

a 22)198

b 45)135

c 56)728

d 54)896

e 29)216

f 73)659

Division and multiplication problems

A **1** Dina's roll of red ribbon is 3 600 cm long. She uses it all to wrap 15 presents, cutting equal lengths of ribbon for each gift. How long is each piece of ribbon?

2 Steve is tying big bows. He has a piece of blue cord 381 cm long, and he cuts it into 23 pieces of equal length with 13 cm left over. How long is the cord for each bow?

3 The Christmas balls arrived in a big box. The box had 48 rows, with 16 balls in a row.
  a How many balls were there altogether?
  b The shopkeeper packaged the balls in boxes of 14. How many boxes did she make, and how many balls were left over?

4 The shopkeeper received a parcel of gold stars. She divided the stars into packs of 12. She had enough stars to make 15 packs, and she had 3 stars left over.
  a How many stars were in the parcel?
  b Which number would we call the remainder?

B Copy these and complete them.
  a ____ × 38 = 3 800
  b ____ × 193 = 1 930
  c ____ × 96 = 960
  d 100 × ____ = 1 000
  e ____ ÷ 10 = 200
  f ____ ÷ 100 = 12
  g 1 000 ÷ ____ = 10
  h 20 000 ÷ ____ = 200
  i 41 × ____ = 41 000

Averages

The average of a set of quantities = $\dfrac{\text{sum of the quantities}}{\text{number of the quantities}}$

This table shows how ten pupils scored in their science test.

Name	Jenny	Linda	George	Leslie	Dick	Andy	Jill	Terence	Gina	Sally
Scores out of 30	20	17	25	29	30	21	19	22	30	24

The sum of their scores = 20 + 17 + 25 + 29 + 30 + 21 + 19 + 22 + 30 + 24 = 237.
The number of quantities is the number of scores: 10.

$$= \dfrac{\text{sum of the quantities}}{\text{number of the quantities}} \quad = \dfrac{237}{10}$$
$$= 237 \div 10$$
$$= 23.7$$

The average score is 23.7.

A Jill saved some money each month. This is how much she saved each month for a year.

January	February	March	April	May	June
$8.00	$9.00	$7.00	$7.00	$5.00	$6.00

July	August	September	October	November	December
$10.00	$8.00	$9.00	$6.00	$7.00	$8.01

1. What was Jill's average saving for the first six months?

2. What was Jill's average saving for the last six months?

3. You should be able to work out Jill's average for the two-month period of March and April without any calculations.
   a. What is the average?
   b. Explain how you knew the answer to question a.

B Work out the average of each set of numbers.
   a. 3, 14, 26, 37, 43, 51   b. 9, 6, 28, 32, 60   c. 15, 90, 89, 67, 56

C 1. Work out the average age of students in your class.

2. Measure the heights (in centimetres) of the students in your class. Record the information in a table.

3. Use the information from question 2 to answer these questions.
   a. What is the average height of the boys?
   b. What is the average height of the girls?
   c. What is the average height of the whole group?

Assessment

C

1 Say whether each statement is true or false.
   a A prime number is always odd.
   b 9 is a prime number.
   c A number with only two factors is a prime number.
   d There are five prime numbers between 1 and 10.

2 For each example, would the answer be odd or even?
   a odd + odd   b even + even   c odd + even   d odd × odd

3 The grandfather clock chimes every 5 minutes. The travelling clock chimes every 12 minutes, and the cuckoo clock chimes every 16 minutes. After how many minutes will the clocks chime together?

4 Copy each sequence. Write the next three numbers in each. State what rule you used to find the next three numbers in each case.
   a 7, 11, 15, 19   b 3, 10, 17, 24   c 260, 271, 282, 293
   d 392, 389, 386, 383   e 975, 950, 925, 900   f 30, 55, 80, 105
   g 134, 128, 122, 116

B

1 Find the HCF of these numbers.
   a 28, 42   b 16, 20, 32   c 15, 27   d 45, 60   e 52, 39

2 Write number sentences for the following problems, and work out the answers.
   a 8 700 students wrote an examination. If 6 948 students were girls, how many boys wrote the examination?
   b A farmer sold 450 boxes of oranges, 1 732 boxes of plums, 1 864 boxes of mangoes and 399 boxes of limes. How many boxes did the farmer sell altogether?
   c A box contains 13 rows of eggs with 14 eggs in each row. The shopkeeper rearranges the eggs in a different box, in rows of 7. How many eggs are now in each row?

Fractions

You have already learned about writing fractions, and solving problems using fractions. A fraction is a way of expressing a number or amount that has been divided into parts. There are many ways of expressing fractions.

$$3 \div 5 \ = \ \frac{3}{5} \ = \ \text{(pie chart)} \ = \ 0.6$$

In this chapter, you will practise adding, subtracting, multiplying and dividing fractions.

Review of fractions

A **1** a Copy this table, and fill in the correct words in column 3: proper fraction, improper fraction or mixed number.

b Then draw the missing pictures and fill in the missing fractions.

Picture	Fraction	Description
(circle divided in thirds, one shaded)	$\frac{2}{3}$	proper fraction
	$\frac{13}{8}$	
	$3\frac{7}{9}$	
(three squares)		mixed number
(diamond shape)	$\frac{7}{8}$	
	$\frac{9}{10}$	proper fraction

2 Turn these improper fractions into mixed numbers:

a $\frac{11}{3}$ b $\frac{19}{3}$ c $\frac{145}{12}$

3 Turn these mixed numbers into improper fractions:

a $3\frac{3}{4}$ b $5\frac{1}{2}$ c $8\frac{1}{4}$

Reciprocals

$3 \div 1 = 3$. So another way of writing 3 is $\frac{3}{1}$.

To find the reciprocal, interchange the denominator with the numerator.

So the reciprocal of 3 (or $\frac{3}{1}$) is $\frac{1}{3}$. The reciprocal of 18 is $\frac{1}{18}$.

4 Write down the reciprocals for each number.
a 6   b 10   c 24   d 17   e 9

5 Use these numbers: 1, 2, 3, 7, 9, 12.
a Write as many proper fractions as you can.
b Write as many improper fractions as you can.
c Write as many mixed numbers as you can.
d Convert the mixed numbers in c to improper fractions.
e Convert the improper fractions in b to mixed numbers.

Lowest common denominator

The lowest common denominator (LCD) of a set of fractions is the lowest common multiple (LCM) of their denominators. For example:
Find the LCD of $\frac{1}{2}, \frac{1}{4}, \frac{5}{6}$.

The denominators are: 2, 4, 6. The LCM is 12.
The LCD is 12.

We can re-write the fractions using the LCD. This helps us to compare the fractions.

$\frac{1}{2} = \frac{6}{12}$ $\frac{1}{4} = \frac{3}{12}$ $\frac{5}{6} = \frac{10}{12}$

Can you see which fraction is biggest and which fraction is smallest? $\frac{1}{2} > \frac{1}{4} < \frac{5}{6}$

A Copy and complete this table. The first example has been done for you.

	Fractions	LCM of denominators	LCD of fractions	Fractions written with LCD
a	$\frac{1}{5}, \frac{1}{4}$	20	20	$\frac{4}{20}, \frac{5}{20}$
b	$\frac{2}{5}, \frac{3}{10}, \frac{1}{15}$			
c	$\frac{1}{4}, \frac{1}{10}, \frac{2}{3}$			
d	$\frac{3}{2}, \frac{3}{4}, \frac{3}{8}$			
e	$\frac{3}{7}, \frac{2}{3}, \frac{5}{4}$			

B

1 Write each of these pairs using the LCD. Then write $<$, $>$ or $=$ for each pair.
a $\frac{1}{2}, \frac{8}{12}$ b $\frac{1}{2}, \frac{5}{8}$ c $\frac{1}{4}, \frac{2}{10}$ d $\frac{3}{12}, \frac{1}{4}$ e $\frac{3}{6}, \frac{1}{4}$ f $\frac{3}{5}, \frac{2}{3}$

2 Write each of the following sets as fractions using the LCD of each set.
a $\frac{10}{11}, \frac{4}{5}$ b $\frac{1}{6}, \frac{3}{8}$ c $\frac{2}{9}, \frac{1}{3}, \frac{5}{6}$ d $\frac{17}{42}, \frac{13}{14}, \frac{3}{4}$

Using the lowest common denominator

A

1 Find the LCD of each set of fractions, then arrange each set in order of size, from smallest to largest.

a $\frac{1}{2}, \frac{1}{5}, \frac{1}{3}, \frac{1}{4}$

b $\frac{5}{9}, \frac{5}{3}, \frac{5}{4}, \frac{5}{12}$

2 Look at your answers to question 1. What is an easy way of ordering fractions with the same numerator?

B

1 Arrange each set of fractions in order of size, in descending order.

a $\frac{1}{11}, \frac{1}{7}, \frac{1}{6}, \frac{1}{8}$ b $\frac{2}{5}, \frac{2}{9}, \frac{2}{13}, \frac{2}{3}$

c $\frac{1}{2}, \frac{2}{3}, \frac{1}{4}, \frac{3}{7}$ d $\frac{5}{9}, \frac{1}{3}, \frac{5}{6}$

2 Arrange each set of fractions in ascending order.

a $\frac{5}{18}, \frac{5}{7}, \frac{5}{11}, \frac{5}{6}$

b $\frac{7}{8}, \frac{7}{40}, \frac{7}{9}, \frac{7}{20}$

c $\frac{11}{16}, \frac{1}{4}, \frac{3}{5}, \frac{9}{10}$

d $\frac{11}{12}, \frac{1}{2}, \frac{5}{8}, \frac{7}{6}$

C

1 $\frac{1}{2}$ and $\frac{4}{8}$ are equivalent fractions. This is because $\frac{4}{8}$ can be simplified, using the LCD, to make $\frac{1}{2}$. Use the LCD to help you work out which fractions in each list are equivalent.

a $\frac{1}{2}, \frac{1}{4}, \frac{2}{4}, \frac{6}{12}, \frac{6}{10}$

b $\frac{1}{5}, \frac{3}{5}, \frac{5}{6}, \frac{6}{10}, \frac{30}{50}$

c $\frac{18}{20}, \frac{4}{9}, \frac{9}{10}, \frac{45}{50}, \frac{9}{20}$

2 Which fraction is halfway between $\frac{1}{3}$ and $\frac{5}{6}$?

3 Copy and complete these equivalent fractions.

a $\frac{4}{9} = \frac{32}{\square}$ b $\frac{7}{12} = \frac{\square}{144}$ c $\frac{9}{13} = \frac{63}{\square}$ d $\frac{3}{\square} = \frac{12}{20}$

e $\frac{8}{\square} = \frac{2}{5}$ f $\frac{9}{27} = \frac{1}{\square}$ g $\frac{\square}{50} = \frac{4}{100}$ h $\frac{36}{54} = \frac{3}{\square}$

Adding fractions

It is easy to add fractions with the same denominators.
For example: $\frac{3}{7} + \frac{1}{7} = \frac{4}{7}$

When you want to add two fractions with different denominators, you need to find the LCD.

$\frac{4}{5} + \frac{1}{2} + \frac{2}{3}$

$= \frac{24}{30} + \frac{15}{30} + \frac{20}{30}$

$= \frac{59}{30}$

$= 1\frac{29}{30}$

$2\frac{1}{4} + 1\frac{5}{6}$

$= \frac{9}{4} + \frac{11}{6}$

$= \frac{27}{12} + \frac{22}{12}$

$= \frac{49}{12}$

$= 4\frac{1}{12}$

or $3\frac{3}{12} + \frac{10}{12}$

$= 3\frac{13}{12}$

$= 4\frac{1}{12}$

When you are working with mixed numbers it helps to convert them to improper fractions before you find the LCD to add.

A

 1
a $\frac{8}{9} + \frac{7}{9} + \frac{2}{9}$
b $\frac{5}{8} + \frac{1}{3}$
c $3\frac{4}{5} + 1\frac{1}{6}$
d $\frac{3}{4} + 2\frac{3}{7} + 1\frac{1}{2}$
e $3\frac{1}{7} + 4\frac{2}{3} + \frac{1}{5}$
f $\frac{22}{7} + \frac{5}{4} + \frac{15}{2}$

2
a Find the sum of $4\frac{3}{10}$ and $1\frac{2}{15}$.
b Add $4 + \frac{1}{2}$.
c Find the sum of $1\frac{1}{3}$ and $\frac{2}{15}$.
d Add $2 + \frac{3}{5} + \frac{1}{2}$.
e Find the sum of $4\frac{5}{8}$ and $\frac{3}{4}$.
f Add $7 + 2\frac{1}{2} + \frac{1}{4}$.

B Mrs James baked a round cake. She gave $\frac{1}{3}$ of the cake to Sheila, $\frac{2}{5}$ to Agatha, and $\frac{1}{4}$ to George.

a Who received the largest piece?
b Who received the smallest piece?
c What fraction of the cake was left?

C $\frac{7}{15}$ of the passengers on a plane went to St Lucia. $\frac{1}{6}$ of the passengers went to Trinidad and $\frac{1}{5}$ of the passengers went to Barbados.

a What fraction of the passengers went to St Lucia, Trinidad and Barbados?
b What fraction of the passengers went to other destinations?
c What was the smallest number of seats possible on the aeroplane?
(Hint: use the LCD.)

Subtracting fractions

As in addition, it is easy to subtract fractions with the same denominator.
For example: $\frac{3}{7} - \frac{1}{7} = \frac{2}{7}$

Finding the LCD helps us to find the difference between fractions that have different denominators. For example:

$\frac{4}{5} - \frac{2}{3}$

$= \frac{12}{15} - \frac{10}{15}$

$= \frac{2}{15}$

$2\frac{1}{4} - 1\frac{5}{6}$

$= \frac{9}{4} - \frac{11}{6}$

$= \frac{27}{12} - \frac{22}{12}$

$= \frac{5}{12}$

$2 - \frac{3}{8}$

$= \frac{16}{8} - \frac{3}{8}$

$= \frac{13}{8}$

$= 1\frac{5}{8}$

A **1** Work these out.

a $\frac{11}{16} - \frac{5}{16}$

b $\frac{5}{9} - \frac{1}{4}$

c $4\frac{6}{7} - 2\frac{1}{3}$

d $3\frac{1}{2} - 2\frac{4}{15}$

e $10 - \frac{9}{10}$

f $3 - \frac{1}{3}$

2 Do the following. Give your answers in the simplest form.

a $(\frac{5}{8} - \frac{1}{4}) + \frac{1}{2}$

b $(3\frac{5}{6} - 1\frac{1}{3}) + \frac{1}{2}$

c $(7\frac{7}{10} + \frac{3}{5}) - \frac{1}{2}$

d $(10\frac{7}{8} - 2\frac{1}{3}) + \frac{1}{9}$

e $(1\frac{19}{20} - \frac{1}{5}) + 5\frac{1}{2}$

B a Emily gave her grandmother $\frac{2}{5}$ of a loaf of bread. What fraction of the bread was left?

b If Emily's loaf had 20 slices, how many slices did Emily give her grandmother?

C John gave $\frac{3}{8}$ of a box of plums to his mother, and $\frac{1}{5}$ to his friend. $\frac{3}{10}$ of the box were bad, so he threw them away and ate the rest.

a What fraction of the plums did John give away?

b What fraction did John eat?

Discuss why this rule is important:
When adding or subtracting fractions with unlike denominators, first find the LCD.

Multiplying fractions

There are different methods of multiplying fractions.

For example:

$\frac{3}{4} \times \frac{1}{2}$

$= \frac{(3 \times 1)}{(4 \times 2)}$

$= \frac{3}{8}$

$\frac{5}{6}$ of 12

$= \frac{5}{6_1} \times \frac{\cancel{12}^2}{1}$

$= 5 \times \frac{2}{1}$

$= 10$

$\frac{\cancel{5}^1}{\cancel{8}_4} \times \frac{\cancel{6}^2}{7} \times \frac{\cancel{1}^1}{\cancel{15}_5}$

$= \frac{1}{28}$

$1\frac{3}{4} \times 2\frac{4}{7}$

$= \frac{7}{4} \times \frac{18}{7}$

$= \frac{9}{2}$

$= 4\frac{1}{2}$

A

1 Calculate. Give your answer as proper fractions or mixed numbers.

    a $\frac{3}{10}$ of 250
    b $5\frac{2}{3} \times \frac{3}{4}$
    c $2\frac{1}{3} \times 4\frac{1}{5}$

2   a $\frac{1}{3} \times 2\frac{1}{4} \times \frac{8}{9}$
    b $3\frac{2}{5} \times 4\frac{1}{4} \times \frac{1}{8}$
    c $7 \times \frac{8}{9}$

3   a $\frac{1}{2} \times \frac{3}{5} - \frac{1}{4}$
    b $\frac{11}{12} \times 1\frac{1}{7} + \frac{1}{3}$
    c $(\frac{9}{8} - \frac{5}{6}) \times 1\frac{1}{2}$

B Jenny had 24 grapes. She ate $\frac{1}{3}$ of them and gave $\frac{3}{4}$ of the rest to Tom.

a How many grapes did Jenny eat?
b How many grapes did she give to Tom?
c How many grapes did she have left?

C There are 320 T-shirts in a delivery box. $\frac{1}{5}$ of the T-shirts are red, $\frac{1}{4}$ of the T-shirts are green and $\frac{3}{8}$ of the T-shirts are blue. The rest of the T-shirts are white.

a How many T-shirts are red?
b How many T-shirts are green?
c How many T-shirts are blue?
d What fraction of the T-shirts are white?

D

1   a $\frac{4}{5} \times \frac{2}{2} = \boxed{}$
    b $\frac{6}{7} \times \frac{5}{5} = \boxed{}$
    c $\frac{7}{11} \times \frac{3}{3} = \boxed{}$

2 Look at your answers to question 1. Write a rule about how to create equivalent fractions.

3 Generate five equivalent fractions for each of these fractions.

    a $\frac{10}{11}$
    b $\frac{77}{100}$
    c $\frac{12}{15}$
    d $\frac{19}{25}$

4 Find the value of n.

    a $\frac{1}{2} + \frac{1}{3} = n$
    b $4 \times \frac{2}{3} = n$
    c $2\frac{1}{2} \times 2\frac{1}{2} = n$

Dividing fractions

Fractions can be divided by whole numbers using reciprocals.

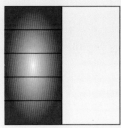

$\frac{1}{2} \div 5 = \frac{1}{10}$

= $\frac{1}{10}$ of the whole.

Remember that a whole number always has 1 as a denominator. 1 is the same as $\frac{1}{1}$, 2 is the same as $\frac{2}{1}$, 3 is the same as $\frac{3}{1}$.

Dividing a fraction by another number is the same as multiplying the fraction by the reciprocal of the number you wanted to divide by. So we express the whole number as a fraction, then invert the fraction (switch the denominator and numerator) to get the reciprocal, and multiply.

So $\frac{1}{2} \div 5 = \frac{1}{2} \div \frac{5}{1} = \frac{1}{2} \times \frac{1}{5}$

$= \frac{1}{10}$

A

1 Find the reciprocals of these whole numbers.

a 3   b 11   c 5   d 144   e 18

2 Express these division problems using the × sign, and then find the answers.

a $\frac{3}{4} \div 2$ b $\frac{7}{8} \div 4$ c $\frac{9}{10} \div 3$ d $\frac{4}{5} \div 10$ e $\frac{9}{2} \div 4$

3 Copy these and fill in the blanks.

a _____ $\div 6 = \frac{1}{2}$ b _____ $\div 9 = \frac{1}{3}$ c _____ $\div 8 = \frac{3}{4}$ d _____ $\div 12 = \frac{2}{3}$

4 Explain how you found the missing numbers in question 3.

Fractions can also be divided by proper fractions.
We must invert the proper fractions so that we can work out division problems.

$\frac{5}{12} \div \frac{2}{3}$

$= \frac{5}{12} \times \frac{3}{2}$

$= \frac{5}{8}$

change operator
invert divisor

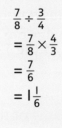

simplify

$\frac{7}{8} \div \frac{3}{4}$

$= \frac{7}{8} \times \frac{4}{3}$

$= \frac{7}{6}$

$= 1\frac{1}{6}$

B

1 Find the reciprocals of these proper fractions.

a $\frac{12}{13}$ b $\frac{2}{3}$ c $\frac{8}{9}$ d $\frac{5}{11}$ e $\frac{5}{18}$

2 Work out these problems.

a $\frac{15}{16} \div \frac{3}{4}$ b $\frac{1}{2} \div \frac{8}{9}$ c $\frac{14}{25} \div \frac{7}{15}$ d $\frac{9}{10} \div \frac{3}{8}$ e $\frac{17}{18} \div \frac{1}{3}$

Mixed numbers can be divided by whole numbers.

$2\frac{1}{2} \div 3 = \frac{5}{2} \div \frac{3}{1}$ change the mixed number to an improper fraction

write the whole number as a fraction with a denominator of 1

$= \frac{5}{2} \times \frac{1}{3}$ change the operator and invert the fraction

$= \frac{5}{6}$

$3\frac{3}{4} \div 9 = \frac{15}{4} \div \frac{9}{1}$ change the mixed number to an improper fraction

write the whole number as a fraction with a denominator of 1

$= \frac{15}{4} \times \frac{1}{9}$ change the operator and invert the fraction

$= \frac{15}{36}$

$= \frac{5}{12}$ simplify the answer

A

1 Write these mixed numbers as improper fractions.

a $1\frac{11}{12}$ b $4\frac{3}{4}$ c $9\frac{9}{10}$ d $11\frac{10}{11}$ e $7\frac{1}{8}$

2 Find the answers.

a $4\frac{1}{3} \div 6$ b $3\frac{1}{5} \div 5$ c $2\frac{9}{11} \div 3$ d $5\frac{1}{4} \div 7$

Fractional problems

$\frac{2}{3}$ of the students in a class are boys. If there are 12 boys in the class, how many students are in the class altogether?

$\frac{2}{3}$ represents 12.

So $\frac{3}{3}$ represents $12 \div \frac{2}{3} = 12 \times \frac{3}{2} = 18$.

There are 18 students in the class.

B

1 Susan has a bag of apples. $\frac{3}{4}$ of the apples are rotten. If 36 apples are rotten, how many apples does Susan have altogether?

2 In a class, $\frac{3}{4}$ of the students in a class are girls. There are 28 boys.

a What fraction of the class are boys?

b How many students are in the class?

3 On a BWIA flight, $\frac{2}{3}$ of the passengers are from Trinidad. If there are 189 passengers altogether, how many were from Trinidad?

Decimals

The decimal system is a place value system with base 10. The base is the number of single-digit numbers in a number system. We have ten single digits (0 to 9). We use a decimal point to show the change in place value from whole numbers to fractions. The word 'deci' means one ten. In this chapter, you will work with two decimal places only.

100s	10s	1s	.	10ths	100ths
4	1	6	.	2	8

The value of the 2 in the example above is = $\frac{2}{10}$ or 0.2.

The value of the 8 in the example above is = $\frac{8}{100}$ or 0.08.

A **1** Write these numbers using decimals.
 a one and four-tenths
 b nine and thirteen-hundredths
 c three and four hundredths
 d eight point seven nine
 e one point zero five
 f eighteen point zero eight

2 Find the value of the 5 in each of the following decimals. Write your answer as a proper fraction and as a decimal.
 a 0.05
 b 50.22
 c 98.75
 d 144.56
 e 22.15

B Copy the table and write the value of the circled digit in words and as a fraction.

Decimal	Value in words	Value as a fraction
0.5⑥	six-hundredths	$\frac{6}{100}$
55.⑥2		
0.⓪1		
90 000.①5		
150.9⑨		

Decimals are found in many places in our daily lives. For example in prices, on petrol pump gauges, on car odometers and in sports times. Work in pairs to make a list of at least 10 other examples of decimals in our daily lives.

Rounding off decimals

A You have already learned how to round off using whole numbers. To round off decimals you apply the same principles.

1. Round off to the nearest whole number.
   a 805.6 b 6 095.1 c 2.8 d 300.9 e 674.3 f 8 105.7

2. Round off to the nearest tenth.
   a 342.82 b 609.172 c 65.519 d 819.086 e 80.043 f 403.28

3. Insert <, > or = between these pairs of decimals to make the sentences true.
   a 6.4   6.04   b 6.04   6.44   c 6.40   6.4   d 6.44   6.40
   e 5.2   5.20   f 5.22   5.02   g 5.02   5.2   h 5.22   5.20

B

1. a Is the man correct? Why or why not?
   b Why do people round off their height, age or weight?

2. With a friend, make a list of three situations when you need to find an accurate measurement and three situations when a rounded off measurement will be accurate enough.

C Ordering decimals

1. The drawing shows you the heights of trees in the Botanical Gardens in Port of Spain. List the trees in order from tallest to shortest.

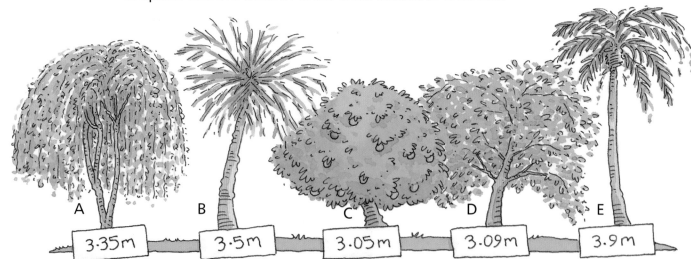

A 3.35m   B 3.5m   C 3.05m   D 3.09m   E 3.9m

2. Place the following decimals in order of size, starting with the smallest.
   a 1.98, 0.19, 0.98, 19.8, 0.09, 0.89
   b 6.77, 7.77, 7.78, 9.11, 1.99, 0.177
   c 0.01, 0.02, 0.11, 0.1, 0.9
   d 7.65, 7.17, 1.99, 2.70, 6.59

Decimals and fractions

You can express fractions as decimals by first converting the denominator to a multiple of ten.

$\frac{16}{50} = \frac{32}{100} = 0.32$

$2\frac{1}{5} = 2\frac{2}{10} = 2.2$

Also $0.45 = \frac{45}{100} = \frac{9}{20}$

A Copy the table below. Match the ordinary fractions with the correct decimal from the box and fill in the pairs in your table.

Fraction	Decimal

$\frac{11}{25}$ 0.9 $\frac{3}{20}$ $\frac{11}{100}$ 12.4

0.85 $\frac{9}{10}$ 0.15 $\frac{130}{100}$

1.3 $12\frac{2}{5}$ 0.8 $\frac{16}{20}$

$\frac{124}{100}$ 0.11   0.44   1.24 $\frac{85}{100}$

B Maria and Tony are lost in Decimal City. Help them find the path home. Check each number sentence to see if it is true (T) or false (F). If it is true, follow the T arrow; if it is false, follow the F arrow.

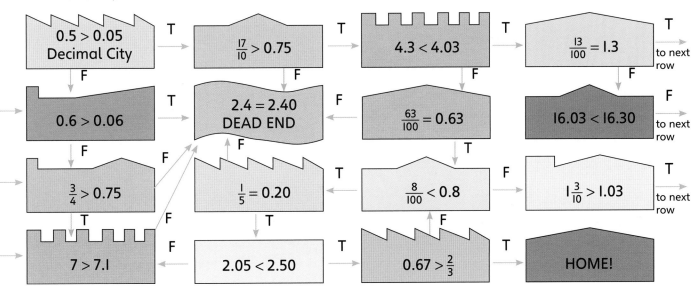

Adding decimals

When you add decimals, always align the decimal points so that you are adding digits with the same place value.

For example:

21.5	21.50	309.57	309.57
3.18	3.18	12.34	12.34
+ 0.92	+ 0.92	+ 8.83	+ 8.83
25.60	25.60	330.74	330.74

The shaded zero shows the empty decimal place. You can add these zeros to help you work out the sum.

A **1** Work out the answer, and then check it using a calculator.

a
```
  3.6
+ 4.2
```

b
```
  5.4
  6.3
+ 9.08
```

c
```
  4.26
  18.1
+ 0.87
```

d
```
  11.20
  15.64
  236.00
+    4
```

2 Work out the answer, and then check it using a calculator.

a 4.8 + 6.1

b 7.5 + 8.46 + 0.9

c 2.148 + 4.25 + 17.6

d 18.92 + 14.06 + 0.72

B At the hardware store, many things are measured in metres and centimetres. Work out the total length of all the labelled items in stock.

WOOD: 3.6m, 2.42m, 1.24m, 1.155m, 1.8117m, 1.76m, 1.12m

Poles

WIRE: 14.99m, 15.112m

ROPE: 6.2m, 7.09m, 5.978m

Subtracting decimals

When you subtract decimals, you must always make sure you align the decimal points
of the numbers so that you are subtracting digits that have the same place value.
For example:

37.68	17.92	4.00
− 24.56	− 16.57	− 0.57
13.12	1.35	3.43

A Subtract these.

1
a   4.8
     − 2.6

b   14.6
     − 11.97

c   10
     − 9.7

d   13.94
     − 10.62

2 Work these out.

a 5.8 − 2.5
b 14.2 − 11.59
c 816.2 − 790.87

d 12 − 9.14
e 15.4 − 12.8
f 13.5 − 10.41

B Work out how much fabric is left on each roll after the piece in front
of it is cut off.

Children	Mass in kg
May	36.06
Paul	38.11
Kit	41.5
Bob	44
Joan	35.92

1 What is the difference in mass between:
   a Bob and May?   b Kit and Joan?   c Paul and May?
   d Bob and Paul?   e Bob and Joan?   f Kit and May?

2 a Between which two children is there the smallest difference in mass?
   b What is the difference in their mass?

3 a Between which two children is there the greatest difference in mass?
   b What is the difference in their mass?

Enrichment activity

A Copy and complete the decimal cross-number puzzle. First solve the across clues. Then solve the down clues and check your answers. You can use a calculator. No numbers should be written in the boxes containing decimal points [•] .

1		2			3
				4	
5			6		
		7			
	8				
9					

Across

1. Add 1.37 to 1.75.
4. Subtract 54.9 from 91.37. Round off your answer to the nearest whole number.
5. Subtract 0.29 from 10.
7. Add 26.85 to 26.87. Round your answer to one decimal place.
9. Find the sum of 3.9, 14.67 and 12.28.

Down

1. Subtract 0.04 from 4.
2. Find the sum of 0.36, 0.78 and 0.61.
3. Find the difference between 100 and 13.26.
6. Add 8.52 to 9.7, and then subtract 4.4. Round your answer to one decimal place.
8. Add 38.6, 20.49 and 30.51. Round your answer to the nearest whole number.

B This game can be played by any number of players.
Draw these boxes on a sheet of paper.

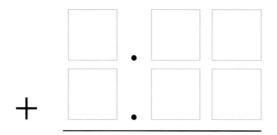

1 Using the digits 2, 3, 4, 5, 8 and 9, write one digit in each box to try and find:
   a the largest total.
   b the smallest total.

2 Draw the boxes again, and replace + with −. Find:
   a the greatest difference.
   b the smallest difference.

Multiplying decimals by powers of ten

A Choose the right words from the ones in brackets.

1 When multiplying a decimal by 10, move the digits in the decimal (one place, two places, three places) to the (left, right).

2 When multiplying a decimal by 100, move the digits in the decimal (one place, two places, three places) to the (left, right).

3 When multiplying a decimal by 1 000, move the digits in the decimal (one place, two places, three places) to the (left, right).

4 When multiplying a decimal by a power of 10, move the digits in the decimal to the (left, right). The number of places = the number of (digits, tens, ones, zeros) in the power of ten.

B

1 Julie has a bug collection. She lines up her caterpillars. Work out how long each line will be if she has 100 of each kind.

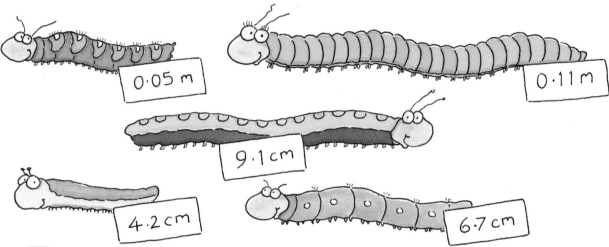

0·05 m   0·11 m   9·1 cm   4·2 cm   6·7 cm

2 Work these out.

a 0.6×100 b 0.15×100 c 3.7×100 d 100×0.8 e 100×0.07

C Copy these and fill in the blanks.

1 a $3.4 \times 10 = \underline{}$ b $0.1 \times 100 = \underline{}$

c $2.04 \times 10 = \underline{}$ d $20.6 \times \underline{} = 20\ 600$

2 Copy these and fill in the blanks.

a $\underline{} \times 100 = 520$ b $0.4 \times \underline{} = 40$

c $0.06 \times 1\ 000 = \underline{}$ d $3.01 \times \underline{} = 3\ 010$

3 To change measurements from centimetres to millimetres, a biologist multiplies them by 10.

a Work out the lengths of these beetles in millimetres.

b Round each millimetre measurement to the nearest whole millimetre.

c Which type of beetle is the longest?

Beetle type	Length in centimetres
Blister	1.48
Colorado	2.53
Golden	2.67
Great Water	3.14
Stag	7.72

Dividing decimals by powers of ten

A Choose the right words from the ones in brackets.

1. When dividing a decimal by 10, move the digits in the decimal (one place, two places, three places) to the (left, right).

2. When dividing a decimal by 100, move the digits in the decimal (one place, two places, three places) to the (left, right).

3. When dividing a decimal by 1 000, move the digits in the decimal (one place, two places, three places) to the (left, right).

4. When dividing a decimal by a power of 10, move the digits in the decimal to the (left, right). The number of places = the number of (digits, tens, ones, zeros) in the power of ten.

B Each coil of rope must be divided into equal parts.
  a Work out the length of the pieces if each coil is divided into 10 equal pieces.
  b Work out the length of the pieces if each coil is divided into 100 equal pieces.

3.4 m   29.1 m   0.3 m   128 m   5 m

C

1. Copy and complete.
   a $2.9 \div \underline{\quad} = 0.29$
   b $\underline{\quad} \div 1\,000 = 3.04$
   c $\underline{\quad} \div 10 = 0.16$
   d $\underline{\quad} \div 10 = 0.69$
   e $3 \div 100 = \underline{\quad}$
   f $140 \div 1\,000 = \underline{\quad}$

2. Work these out.
   a $2.2 \div 10$
   b $39 \div 10$
   c $0.9 \div 10$
   d $680 \div 1\,000$
   e $950 \div 10\,000$
   f $1\,000 \div 10\,000$

3. Work these out.
   a $15.5 \div 10$
   b $13.39 \div 100$
   c $111 \div 100$
   d $23\,988 \div 10$
   e $55\,476 \div 100$
   f $1\,000 \div 1\,000$

4. To find the length in millimetres, a biologist divides centimetre lengths by 10. Find the length of each beetle in millimetres.

a   b   c   d

1.5 cm   1.6 cm   1.4 cm   1.5 cm

Multiplying decimals by whole numbers

When you multiply a decimal by a whole number, the answer always has the same number of decimal places as the decimal. Always remember to put the decimal point in the right place in your answer.

For example:

6.8 × 32

6.8	×	32	=	217.6
↓		↓		↓
decimal tenths		whole number		decimal with one decimal place

```
    6.8
 ×   32
   13.6
  204.0
  217.6
```

1.24 × 16

1.24	×	16	=	19.84
↓		↓		↓
decimal hundreths		whole number		decimal with two decimal places

```
   1.24
 ×   16
   7.44
  12.40
  19.84
```

A

1 Multiply these.
  a 1.5 × 14
  b 14.83 × 15
  c 1.19 × 22

2 Multiply these.
  a 6.2 × 18
  b 15.8 × 25
  c 19.37 × 13

B Find the answers.

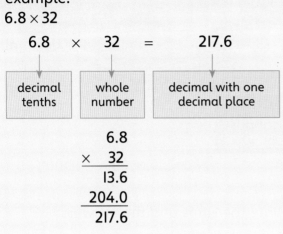

0.45 litres

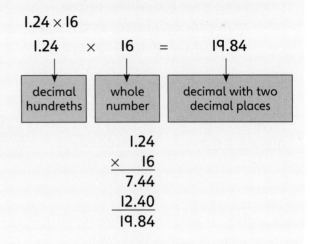

0.25 litres

a How many litres are there in 6 cans?

b How many litres are there in 25 mugs?

1.57 litres

2.5 litres

c How many litres are there in 8 buckets?

d How many litres are there in 15 kettles?

C

1 Jenny bought three pieces of ribbon. Each piece was 0.45 metres. What was the total length of her ribbon?

Decimals

Dividing decimals by whole numbers

Mrs Foster made some toffee. She divided it into ten equal parts or tenths. She cut off $\frac{2}{10}$ or 0.2 of the toffee for herself. She shared the remaining $\frac{8}{10}$ or 0.8 of the toffee among her four children. Each child received $\frac{2}{10}$ or 0.2 of the toffee.

June wrote this sentence and drew a diagram to explain what her mother did:

$0.8 \div 4 = 0.2$

A Draw a diagram to show each division. Write the sums and the answers.

1
  a $0.6 \div 2$
  b $0.6 \div 3$
  c $0.8 \div 2$
  d $0.9 \div 3$
  e $0.24 \div 6$

2
  a $0.12 \div 4$
  b $0.15 \div 5$
  c $0.36 \div 3$
  d $0.18 \div 6$
  e $0.36 \div 4$

B

> $0.12 \div 2 = 0.06$ so $0.06 \times 2 = 0.12$

1 Look at your answers in section A. Use them to help you copy these and work them out.

  a $0.3 \times 2 = \underline{}$
  b $0.4 \times \underline{} = 0.8$
  c $\underline{} \times 3 = 0.9$

  d $4 \times \underline{} = 0.12$
  e $\underline{} \times 0.12 = 0.36$
  f $5 \times \underline{} = 0.15$

C

Two men share six-tenths of a cake equally between themselves. Each received 0.3 of the cake.

$$\begin{array}{r} 0.3 \\ 2\overline{)0.6} \end{array}$$

Eight-tenths of an apple was shared between two girls. Each girl received 0.4 of the apple.

$$\begin{array}{r} 0.4 \\ 2\overline{)0.8} \end{array}$$

1 Work these out.

  a $4\overline{)0.8}$
  b $5\overline{)0.25}$
  c $7\overline{)0.42}$
  d $4\overline{)0.20}$

2 Divide these.

  a $0.24 \div 6$
  b $15.3 \div 3$
  c $2.04 \div 3$
  d $12.16 \div 4$
  e $9.06 \div 3$

Decimals in long division

```
    3.5        26 goes into 91 3 times.              3.14
26 )91          26 × 3 = 78                     14 )43.96
    78          The remainder is 13.                  42
  13.0          Put the decimal point after           1.9
  13.0          the ones column.                       1.4
  00.0          0.5 × 26 = 13.0                       0.56
                There is no remainder.                0.56
                91 ÷ 26 = 3.5                         0.00
```

A Make sure there are the correct number of decimal places in your answers.

1 a 114 ÷ 5   b 11.4 ÷ 5   c 907.92 ÷ 12   d 9 079.2 ÷ 12

2 a 77.76 ÷ 32   b 777.6 ÷ 32   c 838.35 ÷ 15   d 8 383.5 ÷ 15

B What number am I? Work out the number for each of the following.

a If you divide me by 32 you get 3.65.   b I am 5.63 less than 151.37 divided by 7.

c If you multiply me by 9, you get 10.35.   d If you multiply me by 8, you get 11.76.

C 1 Each piece of wood must be cut into the number of equal pieces shown below it. Work out the length of the pieces.

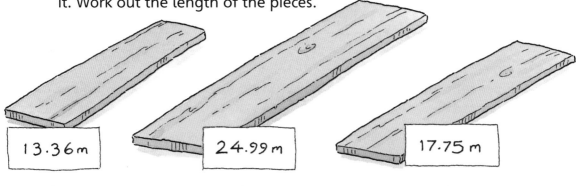

13.36m   24.99 m   17.75 m

a 4 **pieces**   b 3 **pieces**   c 5 **pieces**

2 Each roll of cloth needs to be divided equally into the number of equal pieces shown below it. Work out the length of each piece.

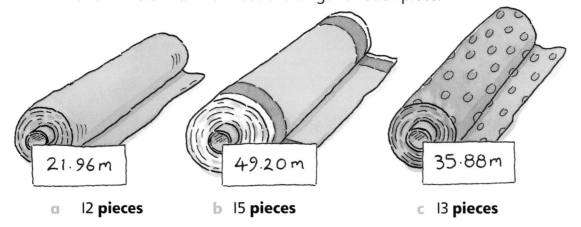

21.96m   49.20 m   35.88m

a 12 **pieces**   b 15 **pieces**   c 13 **pieces**

Percentages

A percentage is a fraction of 100. In this chapter, you will calculate percentages, write percentages as fractions and convert fractions to percentages.

You will also write percentages as decimals, decimals as percentages, and solve real problems using percentages.

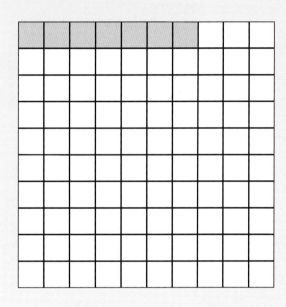

This box shows 100 squares. Each square is $\frac{1}{100}$ of the square. $\frac{1}{100}$ is 1 out of 100 or 1 per cent or 1%. The shaded portion is 7%. The unshaded portion is 93%. Per cent comes from the Latin word centum which means 100.

A　**1**　5 per cent means 5 out of 100. What do each of the following mean?

　　a　6 per cent　　b　90 per cent　　c　10 per cent　　d　100 per cent

2　The symbol % stands for per cent. 3 per cent is usually written as 3%. Write these percentages using the % symbol.

　　a　5 per cent　　b　18 per cent　　c　27 per cent　　d　63 per cent

Converting percentages to fractions
A percentage is a fraction of 100.
For example, $20\% = 20 \div 100 = \frac{20}{100} = \frac{1}{5}$.

$18\% = 18 \div 100 = \frac{18}{100} = \frac{9}{50}$.

$12\frac{1}{2}\% = 12\frac{1}{2} \div 100 = \frac{25}{2} \div \frac{100}{1} = \frac{25}{2} \times \frac{1}{100} = \frac{1}{8}$.

B　Write these percentages as fractions. Simplify your answers to their lowest terms.

　1　a　25%　　b　50%　　c　75%　　d　12%　　e　80%

C　Convert these percentages to fractions in their lowest terms.

　1　a　$55\frac{1}{2}\%$　　b　$32\frac{1}{4}\%$　　c　$33\frac{1}{3}\%$　　d　$37\frac{1}{2}\%$　　e　$42\frac{6}{7}\%$

Fractions and percentages

Converting fractions to percentages
To convert a fraction to a percentage, rewrite the fraction with a denominator of 100.

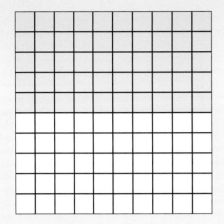

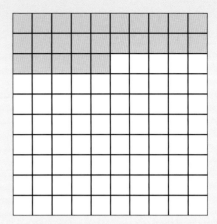

$\frac{1}{2} = \frac{50}{100} = 50$ out of 100

$\frac{1}{2} = 50\%$

$\frac{1}{4} = \frac{25}{100} = 25$ out of 100

$\frac{1}{4} = 25\%$

$\frac{1}{6}$ as a percentage $= 1/6 \times 100 = \frac{100}{6} = \frac{50}{3} = 16\frac{2}{3}$

$\frac{1}{6} = 16\frac{2}{3}\%$

A

1 Draw diagrams to show:

a $\frac{3}{4} = \frac{}{100} = \underline{\quad}\%$

b $1 = \frac{}{100} = \underline{\quad}\%$

2 Copy these and complete them.

a $\frac{1}{5} = \frac{}{100} = \underline{\quad}\%$

b $\frac{3}{5} = \frac{}{100} = \underline{\quad}\%$

c $\frac{7}{10} = \frac{}{100} = \underline{\quad}\%$

d $\frac{13}{50} = \frac{}{100} = \underline{\quad}\%$

e $\frac{6}{25} = \frac{}{100} = \underline{\quad}\%$

f $\frac{3}{20} = \frac{}{100} = \underline{\quad}\%$

B Write these fractions as a percentage.

a $\frac{20}{100}$

b $\frac{8}{10}$

c $\frac{6}{24}$

d $\frac{7}{50}$

e $\frac{3}{5}$

f $\frac{9}{20}$

g $\frac{1}{7}$

h $\frac{5}{8}$

C What percentage of each diagram is shaded?

a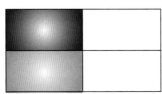

b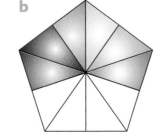

c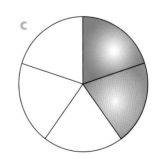

Decimals and percentages

$$0.28 = \frac{28}{100} = 28\% \qquad\qquad 1.6 = \frac{16}{10} = \frac{160}{100} = 160\% \qquad\qquad 45\% = \frac{45}{100} = 0.45$$
$$\text{or } 45 \div 100 = 0.45$$

$$13\tfrac{1}{2} = 13.5 \div 100 = 0.135$$

A Write these percentages as decimals.

1 a 12% b 98% c 2% d 80% e 7% f 100%

2 a $9\frac{9}{10}\%$ b $95\frac{1}{3}\%$ c $5\frac{1}{8}\%$ d $52\frac{3}{5}\%$ e $8\frac{5}{6}\%$

3 a 18.2% b 6.5% c 25.25% d 80.75% e 99.05%

B Write these decimals as percentages.

1 a 0.13 b 0.09 c 0.56 d 0.20 e 0.50 f 0.99

2 a 0.1 b 0.6 c 0.9 d 0.3 e 0.25 f 0.75

3 a 0.44 b 0.02 c 0.22 d 0.01 e 0.04 f 0.14

4 a 0.4 b 0.31 c 0.18 d 0.45 e 0.05 f 0.08

C 1 Write these percentages as decimal fractions.

a 12% b 2% c 10% d 5% e 1% f 20% g 50%

2 Study the diagram, and then copy and complete the table.

Part of diagram shaded	Fraction	Decimal	Per cent
A			
B			
C			
D			

Calculating percentages

Remember, 'per cent' means 'out of 100'. So 3 per cent means 3 out of every 100, and is the same as $\frac{3}{100}$. So 3% of 60 $= \frac{3}{100} \times \frac{60}{1} = \frac{18}{10} = 1\frac{4}{5}$.

We can also work out the total amount if we have a percentage.

For example:

60 is 15% of ___?___.

If 15% represents 60, then 1% represents $\frac{60}{15}$.

So 100% represents $\frac{60}{15} \times 100 = 400$.

A

1 Express your answers as whole numbers or fractions.
   a 2% of 200   b 10% of 600   c 50% of 200   d 20% of 80
   e 75% of 50   f 5% of 40   g 100% of 72   h 15% of 60

2 Now write your answers to question 1 as decimals .
   Use your calculator to check your answers.

3 Write your answers as decimals . Show your working.
   a 10% of 85   b 5% of 171   c 15% of 90
   d 20% of 16   e 15% of 300   f $78\frac{1}{8}$% of 144

B

1 In a school of 400 pupils, 30% are boys.
   a How many boys are there?   b How many girls are there?

2 A fish weighed 6.4 kg. A fishmonger dried it, and it lost 25% of its weight.
   How many kilograms did the fish lose through drying?

3 Copy these and fill in the blanks.
   a 15 is ___% of 30   b 40 is ___% of 80   c 15 is ___% of 45
   d ___% of 50 = 10   e ___% of 80 = 36   f ___% of 120 = 60

4 a What percentage of 50 is 20?   b What percentage of 150 is 90?

C

1 After travelling 40 km, a motorist still has 60% of the journey to travel. What is the total length of the journey?

2 a 50% of a number is 25. What is the number?
   b 45% of a number is 45. What is the number?
   c 80% of John's salary is $48. What is his salary?

3 a Jeremy scored 60% of the total marks on a test. If the test was marked out of 75, what was his score?
   b Sammy was given 75% of a sum of money. If Sammy received $120, what was the total sum of money?

A Problems involving percentages

1 Copy and complete this table.

Item	Original price	Reduction of 20%	Sale price
1 pair ladies' shoes	$80.00		
1 pair gents' shoes			
1 pair boys' shoes			

B

1 The cost of wood went up and a carpenter had to put her prices up by 15%. The picture shows the old prices of the furniture. Work out the new prices and complete the table

Item	Original price	Increase of 15%	New price
large table	$800.00		
set of chairs	$650.00		
small table	$350.00		

C

1 5% of a number is 15. Work out:

  a 50% of the number   b 98% of the number   c 2% of the number

2 29% of a number is 130.5. Work out:

  a 60% of the number   b 2.5% of the number   c 94% of the number

Percentages greater than 100%

My bill increased by almost 200%!

The picture shows Mrs. Brown's reaction when she got this month's electricity bill.
Can you explain her reaction?
Think of two other situations where it is possible to have an increase of more than 100%.

You solve problems involving more than 100% in the same way as you worked before.
For example:

110% of 600   Remember 110% is equivalent to $\frac{110}{100}$

$\frac{110}{100} \times \frac{600}{1} = \frac{66\ 000}{100} = 660$

You can also work out the original amount if you know the percentage amount.
For example:

120% of an amount is 60, what was the original amount?
If 60 = 120% then 1% = $\frac{60}{120}$ = 0.5
If 1% = 0.5 then 100% (the original amount) must be 100 × 0.5 = 50.

Check this by working in reverse:
$\frac{120}{100} \times \frac{50}{1} = \frac{6\ 000}{100} = 60$.

A Calculate:

a 110 % of 500 =
b 125 % of 300 =
c 200 % of 80 =
d 145 % of 1 200 =
e 150 % of 125 =
f 105 % of 260 =

B When businesses sell items they charge more than they paid for the goods. This charge is called a mark up. Some items are sold for more because they are taxed. Calculate the selling price of each item below. Show your working.

a

Cost Price: $60 000
Mark up: 120%

b

Cost Price: $140 000
Mark up: 125%

c

Cost Price: $800
Mark up: 140%

d

Cost Price: $450
Tax: 115%

C Find the value of n.

a 135 % of n = 810
b 120% of n = 300
c 150% of n = 336
d 250 % of n = 920

Assessment

A Sandra goes shopping.

a How much does Sandra pay for the table?

b What is the rate of sales tax in per cent?

c How much is the customs duty on a car valued at $10 000?

B

1 Copy these and complete them.

a ____% of 50 = 10

b ____% of 80 = 36

c ____% of 120 = 60

2 Jerome bought a diary at a discount of 20% and saved $3.60. What was the marked price of the diary?

3 Idetha scored 42 out of 70 on an English examination. What percentage was her score?

4 How much will John save if he buys a $500 bicycle at a discount of 15%?

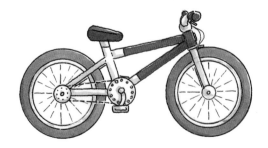

Ratios

A ratio is a kind of fraction. For example, if $\frac{3}{4}$ of your class are right-handed, we could say that 3 out of every 4 children are right-handed and I out of every 4 is left-handed. Or we could say that the ratio of right-handed to left-handed is 3:I.

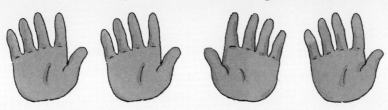

In this chapter, you will learn how to express quantities as ratios.

A In the boxes, you can see how boys and girls are matched in groups – 2 girls for every I boy.

I   How many girls will be matched with:
a   2 boys?   b   4 boys?   c   6 boys?

2   If there are 10 girls, how many boys will there be?

3   How many boys would be matched with 14 girls?

B Joan and Derrick share some money. This is how they share their money.

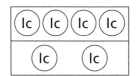 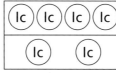 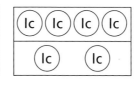 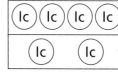 Joan

Derrick

I   a   How much did Joan get?
b   How much did Derrick get?

2   a   If Joan got 40 cents, how much would Derrick get?
b   If Derrick received 16 cents, how much would Joan get?

3:4 is read as '3 to 4'. So if there are 3 girls for every 4 boys in a class, we could say that the ratio of girls to boys is 3 to 4 or 3:4.
We can also say that $\frac{3}{7}$ of the class are girls and $\frac{4}{7}$ are boys.
In a story book, 16 out of every 20 pages have pictures. So the ratio of picture pages to all of the pages is 16:20. $\frac{16}{20} = \frac{4}{5}$. So $\frac{4}{5}$ of the pages have pictures.

C Write these ratios as fractions in their simplest form.
a   6:18   b   10:25   c   20:35   d   24:36

Ratios

Remember, a ratio is a way of expressing a fraction. Just as we have equivalent fractions, we also have equivalent ratios.

$$\frac{3}{4} = \frac{6}{8} = \frac{9}{12} = \frac{12}{16}$$ **OR** $3:4 = 6:8 = 9:12 = 12:16$

A

1. Write five equivalent ratios for each of the following.
   a 2:5   b 1:2   c 4:7   d 7:8   e 4:5

2. Copy and complete.
   a 11:12 = ____ :36   b ____ :3 = 10:15   c 9:11 = ____ :33   d 7:8 = ____ :56

B Copy and complete these ratios, filling in the ratio in its simplest terms.
   a 5:15 = ____ : ____   b 8:12 = ____ : ____   c 4:16 = ____ : ____
   d 18:24 = ____ :12 = ____ : ____   e 24:36 = ____ : ____ = 6: ____

C You can increase or enlarge the size of a picture using a photocopier. Most copiers can be set to reduce or enlarge by a percentage.

1. Maria has copied a page at 75%. This means her copy is 75% or $\frac{3}{4}$ of the original size. She has reduced it so the ratio of the copy to the original is 3:4. What is the ratio of the copy to the original when you reduce by:
   a 50%   b 20%   c 80%

2. What happens to the area shown on the map as the ratio scale decreases?

1:150 000

1:300 000

1:600 000

More ratios

A

1 There are 3 girls for every 2 boys at a party.
   a Draw boxes to show the ratio of boys to girls.
   b There are 20 boys at the party. How many girls are there?

2 A recipe for 20 muffins uses 2 eggs. How many eggs are needed for:
   a 40 muffins?   b 10 muffins?   c 50 muffins?

3 Pam ate 9 nuts in 6 minutes. If she continued eating at the same rate, how many would she eat in:
   a 12 minutes?   b 4 minutes?   c 1 hour?

B

1 It takes a carpenter 5 days to build 8 tables. If the carpenter continues working at the same rate, work out:
   a How many tables can be built in 20 days?
   b How many days does it take to build 24 tables?

2 A man makes 10 fish pots in a day. How long will he take to make 35 fish pots if he works at the same rate?

3 In two days, a seamstress sews 9 dresses. How many days will she take to sew 36 dresses if she works at the same rate?

Cooking sets: include frying pan, saucepan and cooking pan, with soup pot and small pot. All for $200.00!

Special: $1.25 for four water glasses!

Special: buy 3 bowls, get 2 cups!

C

1 How many water glasses could you buy for $10.00?

2 The shopkeeper has 75 large teapots and 45 small teapots in stock. What is the ratio of large teapots to small teapots?

3 A restaurant owner bought 18 bowls. How many free cups did he receive?

4 What is the ratio of pans to pots in each cooking set?

Calculating ratios

A **1** Jill and Sarah are carrying newspapers from their classroom to the recycling depot. There are 20 bundles of newspapers in the classroom. On each trip, Jill carries 3 bundles and Sarah carries 2 bundles.

    a How many trips did the girls make to carry all 20 bundles to the depot?
    b How many bundles of newspaper did each girl carry in total?

    2 Jill's class also collects old magazines to take to the nearby hospital. For every 2 magazines that go into the small collection box, 4 magazines go into the big collection box. One week, the children collect 210 magazines.

    a Draw a diagram to show how the magazines are shared between the collection boxes.
    b How many magazines went into each box?

B Jennifer and Sam went picking mangoes. Jennifer could pick 11 mangoes in the time that Sam took to pick 7 mangoes. When they went home, they had a total of 36 mangoes. How many mangoes did each pick?

C Paula and Jonathan shared 51 mangoes. Paula got twice as many as Jonathan.
  a Draw boxes to show each child's share.
  b What was Paula's share?
  c What was Jonathan's share?

Chapter 8 Money

In this chapter, you will perform various operations on money and will study various concepts associated with money, such as profit and loss, foreign exchange, discounts and hire purchase.

When we write amounts of money, the decimal point is always between the dollars and the cents.
$9 807 241.15 is read as 'nine million, eight hundred and seven thousand, two hundred and forty-one dollars and fifteen cents'. Note that we do not write 'c' in dollar amounts.

A

1 Write the following amounts in words.

a

$215 600 · 00

b

$8 061 918 · 00

c

$1 000 754 · 00

2 Write the following in figures.
a Three million and two dollars.
b Three hundred and twenty-five thousand dollars and fifty cents.
c Two million and twenty-five thousand dollars and seven cents.

B

1 Five classes sold fudge to raise money for charity. This is how much they made in a day.

A $15.35   B $27.46   C $14.68   D $32.77   E $19.92

2 a Write the amounts in order from least to most.
b How much more did Class A collect than Class C?
c How much more did Class D collect than Class E?

2 If Classes A and B pool their money together, how much do they have altogether?

3 The local animal shelter needs $60.00 to finish building a new set of kennels. Two of the classes put their money together and had enough to pay for the kennels.
a Which two classes paid for the kennels? How did you work this out?
b How much change did they have?

C

1 Find the sum.
a $2.35 + $6.58   b $16.39 + $12.47   c $48.95 + $12.25   d $173.69 + $89.35

2 Find the difference.
a $4.09 – $2.06   b $7.20 – $5.85   c $31.09 – $18.25   d $129.35 – $106.27

Money problems

A Go to a clothing store, or look at an advertisement in a newspaper. Find prices for the following items:

pair of jeans   pair of sneakers   cap

pair of shoes   T-shirt   shorts

1 Estimate, to the nearest dollar, the totals of these shopping lists.
  a Two pairs of sneakers and a T-shirt
  b Three pairs of jeans and four pairs of shoes
  c Six caps and a pair of shorts

2 a Use your calculator to help you work out the actual total for each list.
  b Describe which notes and coins you could use to pay for each list without getting change.
  c Describe the smallest number of notes you could use to pay for each list, and say how much change you would get.

B Look at the menu for the Green Dragon Chinese Restaurant.

1 Jackie bought soup, six spring rolls and fried rice with vegetables.
  a What did her bill come to?
  b She paid with $40.00. How much change did she get?

2 Simone and Daniel ordered 3 spring rolls, chicken chow mein, prawn noodles and 4 fortune cookies.
  a How much did their bill come to?
  b How much change would they get from $50.00?

3 Imagine you are eating at the Green Dragon. Choose three items from the menu.
  a Estimate the total for your bill.
  b Now work out the exact total. How close were you?
  c Write down which notes and coins you would use to pay for your bill exactly.

Soup $9.99
Spring rolls $6.99 for three
Lunch special $19.75 includes soup, meat, fried rice or chow mein
Lunch box special $9.55 includes meat with rice or chow mein
Fried rice with vegetables $12.85
Chicken chow mein $21.99
Prawn noodles $8.69
Fortune cookies $2.00 each

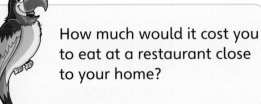

How much would it cost you to eat at a restaurant close to your home?

More money problems

Earlier you learned about percentages. Many shops offer discounts in percentages. For example, Linda went shopping for shoes in Jamaica. The shop was offering a 25% discount on the shoes she liked. The original price was $520.00. How much would Linda have to pay for the shoes?

25% of $520 = $\frac{25}{100}$ of $520.00 or 0.25 × $520.00

$\qquad\qquad$ = $130.00

Amount Linda would pay ➡ $520.00 – $130.00 = $390.00

A **1** Work out the sale prices of each pair of shoes.

a Original price: $590.00
Discount in sale: 35%

b Original price: $675.00
Discount in sale: 30%

c Original price: $695.00
Discount in sale: 15%

d Original price: $845.00
Discount in sale: 42%

e Original price: $499.00
Discount in sale: 25%

2 Use your calculator to check your answers to question 1.

3 For each of the pairs of shoes above, find the difference between the original price and the sale price.

Profit and loss

Profit = selling price – cost price   Loss = cost price – selling price
If the selling price is lower than the cost price, the difference is called the loss, because the seller loses money. Sometimes a seller will sell things at a loss in order to get rid of unwanted stock.

A Copy this table and fill in the missing blanks.

Item	Cost price	Selling price	Profit
Giant fluffy bear		$129.99	$74.99
Mini fluffy bear	$25.00	$49.99	
Train set	$320.00		$439.99
Bat and ball	$15.00	$29.99	
Baby doll		$115.00	$65.00

B **1** Work out whether each of the following items was sold for a profit or a loss, and how much the profit or loss was.

	Cost price	Selling price	Profit or loss
a	$5.00	$8.00	
b	$10.00	$9.99	
c	$35.00	$45.99	
d	$15.75	$29.89	
e	$95.90	$85.99	

2 Lulu runs a shop in St Vincent. She bought 16 bottles of apple jelly at $6 a bottle and sold ten of these bottles for $15 each. Since she needed to sell the apple jelly before the expiry date, she sold the rest of the bottles at a 50% discount.
a What was the total cost price of the jelly?
b How many bottles did Lulu discount?
c What was the total selling price of the discounted bottles of jelly?
d What was the total selling price of all the jelly?
e Work out whether Lulu made a profit or a loss, and how much it was.

C A shopkeeper in Dominica pays $60 for a hand-sewn doll. He sells the dolls for $45.
a What is the cost price of five dolls?
b What is the selling price of five dolls?
c Calculate the loss he made.
d Find the percentage loss.

D **1** A radio costs $400.00. It was sold at a 12.5% profit. Find the selling price.

2 A rug was sold for $180.00 with a loss of 10%.
a What was the cost price?
b Find the loss made.

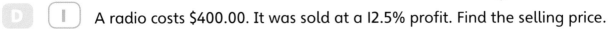

Foreign exchange

Different countries use different kinds of money. These are called currencies. Some currencies used in the Caribbean are: East Caribbean dollar, Barbadian dollar, Jamaican dollar, United States dollar. There are eight other currencies in use in the Caribbean. Find out their names.

US$1.00 = BDS$2.00
How much US currency do you need to buy BDS$250.00?

$250.00 ÷ $2.00 = $125.00
You would need US$125.00

BDS$1.00 = EC$1.35
How much EC currency do you need to buy BDS $150.00?

$150.00 × 1.35 = EC $202.50
You would need EC $202.50

A

1. How much US currency do you need to buy:
   a BDS$101.00   b BDS$184.00   c BDS$349.38

2. How much EC currency do you need to buy:
   a BDS$5.00   b BDS$26.00   c BDS$45.00

3. US $1.00 = EC$2.65. Copy these and complete them:
   a US$7.00 = EC$____   b US$120.00 = EC$____

B

Hire purchase

1. Mr. Joseph buys a refrigerator on hire purchase. He pays the debt off in 20 equal monthly payments. If the hire purchase price is $4 500.00, how much does Mr. Joseph pay each month?

2. A television set costs $1 200.00 if you pay cash. Mrs Brown buys it on hire purchase. She pays a 25% deposit and 12 equal monthly payments of $180.00 per month. Find:
   a the deposit paid
   b the hire purchase price
   c the difference between the hire purchase price and the cash price

C Find out the exchange rate from your currency to each of the following currencies.
   a US dollar   b Euro   c Australian dollar

Assessment

A

1 Order each set of fractions from largest to smallest.

a $\frac{2}{5}, \frac{1}{3}, \frac{3}{4}, \frac{4}{5}, \frac{1}{2}$

b $\frac{1}{12}, \frac{3}{5}, \frac{1}{6}, \frac{2}{3}, \frac{1}{10}$

c $\frac{5}{6}, \frac{9}{10}, \frac{11}{12}, \frac{4}{5}, \frac{2}{3}$

2 Order these decimals from smallest to largest.

a 3.214, 2.431, 2.341, 2.413, 3.124

b 0.09, 0.1, 0.3, 0.03, 0.23

c 0.21, 0.011, 0.08, 0.5, 0.22

3 Work out the value of:

a 40% of 100

b 50% of 300

c 90% of 500

d 100% of 120

e 75% of 400

4 Express 40 as a percentage of 200.

B

1 Which of these has 8 in the tenths place?

a 85.4

b 0.862

c 80

d 35.18

e 875.2

2 Find the sum.

a $\frac{1}{4} + \frac{1}{5}$

b $\frac{1}{3} + \frac{11}{12}$

c $\frac{1}{7} + \frac{2}{3}$

d $\frac{4}{5} + \frac{1}{3}$

e $1\frac{1}{5} + 6\frac{7}{8}$

3 Find the difference.

a $1\frac{2}{3} - \frac{3}{4}$

b $5\frac{1}{6} - 2\frac{7}{8}$

c $6\frac{3}{8} - 5\frac{1}{2}$

d $3\frac{7}{9} - 1\frac{3}{4}$

C

1 Find the product.

a $2\frac{5}{8} \times 1\frac{3}{7}$

b $1\frac{1}{9} \times 7\frac{1}{5}$

c $2\frac{5}{7} \times 8\frac{2}{5}$

2 Find the quotient.

a $4\frac{1}{2} \div 3$

b $1\frac{4}{9} \div 8$

c $\frac{12}{25} \div 4$

d $\frac{127}{150} \div 5$

Assessment

 A

1   Copy these and give the next three numbers in each sequence.
- a   4.05, 4.06, 4.07, ____ , ____ , ____
- b   98.6, 98.7, 98.8, ____ , ____ , ____
- c   0.10, 0.11, 0.12, ____ , ____ , ____
- d   48.16, 48.17, 48.18, ____ , ____ , ____

2   Find the answers.
- a $9.3 - 6.8$
- b $13.43 + 0.5 + 4.26 + 3.2 + 36.99$
- c $11.5 - 7.9 + 5.1$
- d $40 - 17.8$

3   Find the answers.
- a $2\frac{1}{2} + 7\frac{3}{4}$
- b $2\frac{1}{6} + 1\frac{3}{4} + 3\frac{2}{3}$
- c $10\frac{7}{8} - 4\frac{3}{8}$
- d $8\frac{1}{3} - 2\frac{5}{9}$

4   Copy these and complete them.
- a $\frac{1}{2} = \frac{12}{\square} = \frac{\square}{36}$
- b $\frac{24}{\square} = \frac{6}{8} = \frac{\square}{4}$

B

1   Write these as decimals.
- a $\frac{8}{10}$
- b $\frac{3}{100}$
- c $2\frac{1}{10}$
- d $1\frac{5}{100}$
- e $\frac{2}{5}$
- f $2\frac{1}{4}$

2
- a   Write 2.1 as an improper fraction.
- b   Write 88 tenths as a decimal.
- c   Write 4 tenths 8 hundredths as a decimal.
- d   How many hundredths are there in 1.46?

3
- a   The sum of three fractions is $1\frac{5}{6}$. If two of the fractions are $\frac{2}{3}$ and $\frac{1}{2}$, what is the other fraction?

4   Find the answers.
- a   15% of $300
- b   8% of 400 people
- c   75% of 60 oranges
- d   60% of $40
- e   35% of 150 mangoes
- f   12% of $500

5   In a school of 900 students, 46% of the students walk to school and 35% travel by bus. The rest travel by other means.
- a   What percentage of the students travel by other means?
- b   Work out how many students use each mode of transport to school.

6   A Parish Council budgeted $500 000 for refuse removal. At the end of the year they worked out that they had spent 135% of the amount budgeted. How much did they spend on refuse removal?

7   A part-time worker in a shop is paid $25 per hour. She is offered the choice between an increase of 20% per hour or an increase of $7 per hour.
- a   Which option should she take?
- b   A different worker is paid $40 per hour. She is given the same choice (20% or $7 per hour). Which offer is better for her?

Assessment

1. Mrs John spends $\frac{1}{3}$ of her monthly salary on rent, $\frac{1}{4}$ on groceries, and $\frac{1}{12}$ on other bills. She saves the rest. If she saves $800, what is her monthly salary?

Salary advice		June
Employee: Sarah Johns		003621
Payment type: monthly/direct		
Month	**Hours worked**	**Rate**
June	120 hours	$20.00
Total due:		

$4 + 3 + 1 = \frac{8}{12}$ $\qquad$ $\frac{4}{12} = 800$

$\therefore \frac{1}{12} = 200$

2. Mr Smith buys a settee on hire purchase. He pays $600 deposit and 12 equal monthly payments of $250. The cash price of the settee is $2 700.

   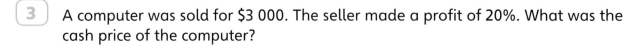

   a What is the hire purchase price?
   b What percentage is the deposit of the hire purchase price?

3. A computer was sold for $3 000. The seller made a profit of 20%. What was the cash price of the computer?

4. Ms James changed BDS$240.00 to EC dollars. If BDS$1.00 = EC$1.35, how much did she receive in EC dollars?

5. If EC$1.00 = TT$2.00, convert the following to EC dollars.
   a TT$750.00
   b TT$381.00
   c TT$95.48

Angles

An angle is formed when two straight lines meet. In this chapter you will learn about different types of angles.

A **1** Make a right angle by folding a piece of paper twice. Use it to find out which of these are right angles.

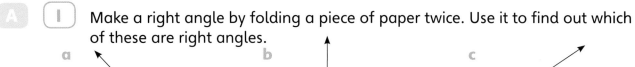

a   b   c

d   e   f

2 Write the names of three objects in your classroom that have right angles.

Angles inside a shape are called interior (meaning 'inside') angles. Angles on the outside of a shape are called exterior angles.

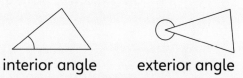

interior angle   exterior angle

B **1** Count all the interior angles.

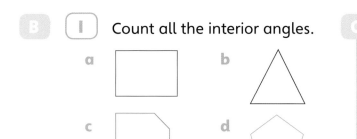

a   b

c   d

C **1** Classify these angles as acute, obtuse, right angle, straight or reflex.

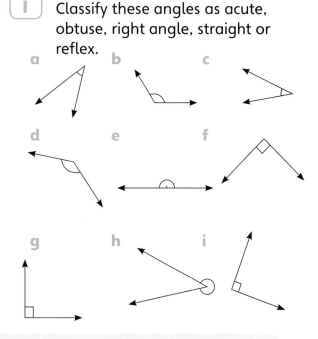

a   b   c

d   e   f

g   h   i

2 Count the number of angles in these diagrams at the point where the two lines meet.

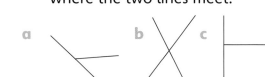

a   b   c

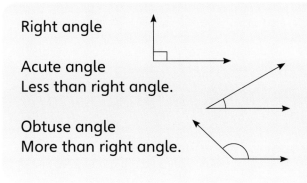

Right angle

Acute angle
Less than right angle.

Obtuse angle
More than right angle.

Straight angle
Straight line/two right angles.

Reflex angle
Bigger than straight angle.

Classifying angles

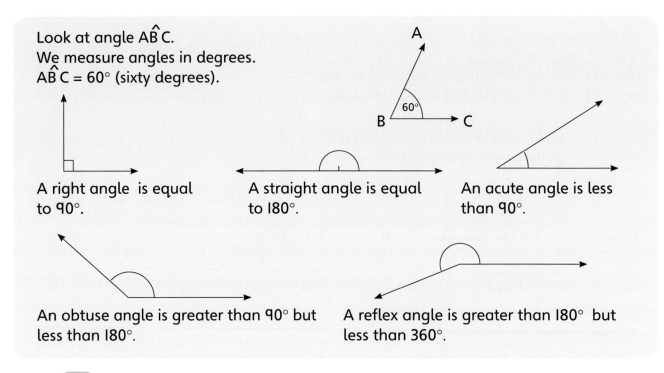

Look at angle AB̂C.
We measure angles in degrees.
AB̂C = 60° (sixty degrees).

A right angle is equal to 90°.

A straight angle is equal to 180°.

An acute angle is less than 90°.

An obtuse angle is greater than 90° but less than 180°.

A reflex angle is greater than 180° but less than 360°.

A **1** Name each angle and classify it as straight, right, acute, obtuse or reflex.

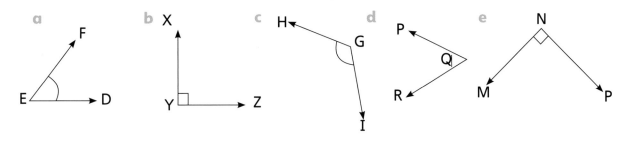

2 Identify which of the angles above are:
a less than 90°
b equal to 90°
c between 90° and 180°
d greater than 180°

B Draw each of the following angles.
a an acute angle
b an obtuse angle
c a straight angle
d a reflex angle
e a right angle

Two right angles = 90° + 90° = 180°.
180° is a straight angle. So a straight angle is equal to two right angles.

Measuring angles

The instrument shown here is a protractor. We use a protractor to measure the size of angles in degrees. Notice that a protractor has two scales – an outer scale and an inner scale. Both scales extend from 0 to 180°. You read the scale from 0. If you start at the 0 on the left hand side of the protractor you read the figures on the inner scale. If you start at the 0 on the right hand side, you use the figures on the outer scale.

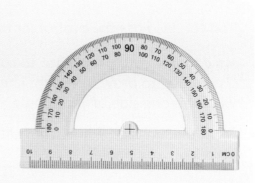

How to measure the size of an angle using a protractor
Find the centre point on the straight edge of the protractor.

Place this point over the vertex, or corner, of the angle you wish to measure.

Line up one of the zero lines on the straight edge of the protractor with one arm of the angle. Keep the centre point on the vertex as you do this.

Find the point where the other arm of the angle intersects the curved edge of the protractor.

Read from 0 using the correct scale to find the number on the scale at the point of intersection. This is the measure of the angle in degrees.

A Look at the two protractors.

a What is the size of each angle shown in the picture?

b What type of angle is ABC?

c What type of angle is EFG?

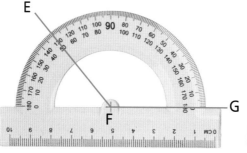

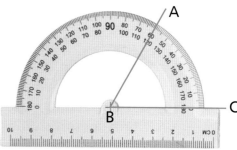

B
1 Estimate the size of each of these angles. Write down your estimate.

2 Use your protractor to measure the size of each angle.

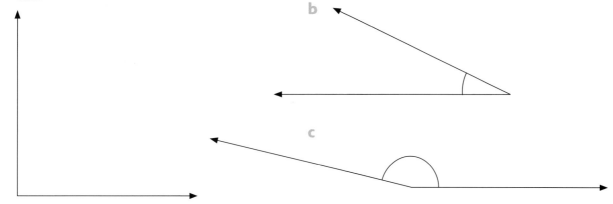

Drawing angles

You can also use the protractor to construct angles.

How to use your protractor to construct an angle
Use a ruler to draw a straight line. This line will form one side of your angle.

Mark a point on the line. This will be the vertex of your angle.

Place the centre point of the protractor over the point you have marked on your line.

Line up the zero on the straight edge of the protractor with the line.

Find the value of your angle on the correct scale of the protractor. Make a mark on the paper at this point.

Use a ruler to connect the mark to the vertex and form an angle.

Rihanna is about to draw an angle. She has marked the number on the curved edge of the protractor that corresponds to the angle she wants to draw. What size angle will this be?

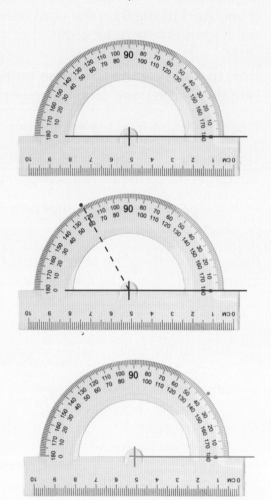

A   Use a ruler and protractor to accurately construct the following angles:
a   70°   b   100°   c   165°   d   30°   e   90°

Discuss how you could construct an angle of 225° using a protractor marked from 0° to 180°.
Try your method.

Playing with angles

A Look at this abstract painting. Work in pairs to complete the activities.

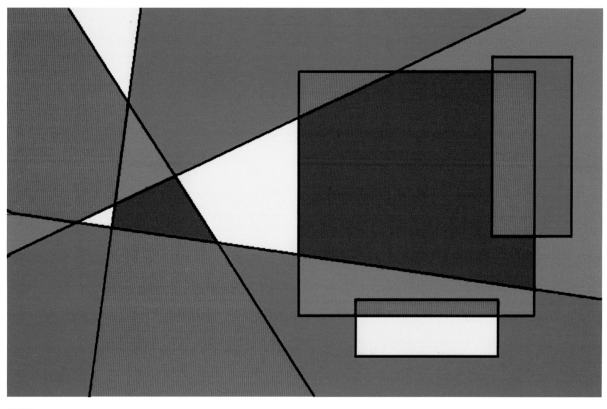

1. How many acute angles can you find in the painting?
2. Estimate the size of each acute angle. Measure each angle to see how well you estimated.
3. Find five obtuse angles in this diagram. Estimate which is biggest and which is smallest. Measure to check whether you estimated correctly.
4. Find two reflex angles in the diagram. Which is smaller? Measure to check your answer.
5. Design and draw a geometric shape painting of your own. Include at least five acute angles, two obtuse angles, three right angles and a reflex angle.

B The diagram below shows all the lines on a tennis court.

1. Copy the diagram into your book and mark all the right angles you can see.
2. Count the right angles. Check with a partner to see if you have missed any.

Chapter 10

Plane shapes

There are many types of plane shapes. In this chapter you will examine some of them and learn about their properties.

A Look at the shapes. Copy the table below. Write the letter of each shape in the correct column.

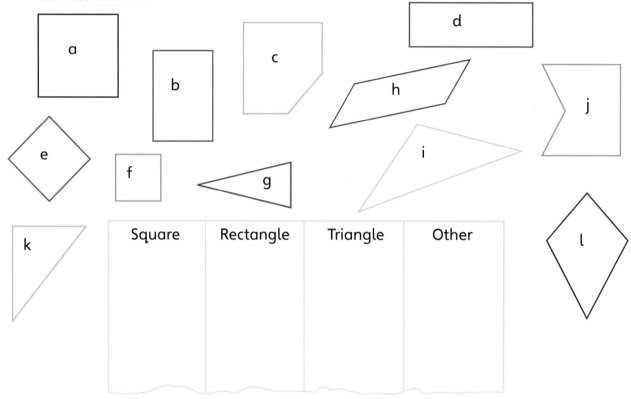

Square	Rectangle	Triangle	Other

B Work with a friend. Look at the figure below. How many different squares, rectangles and triangles can you find?

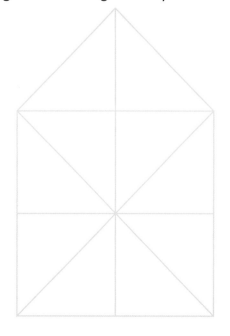

Remember, shapes can overlap!

Revising plane shapes

A **1** Copy and complete this table.

Plane shape	Number of sides	Number of angles	Drawing of the shape
rectangle			
square			
triangle			

2 Say whether each statement is true or false.
a A square has four equal sides.
b Any four-sided figure is a square.
c The opposite sides of a rectangle are equal.
d All triangles have three angles.
e In a square, the width is the longer measure.
f Parallel lines never meet.

B Explain the difference between these two 4-sided shapes.

A

B

C Say whether each shape is a rectangle or a square.

a

b

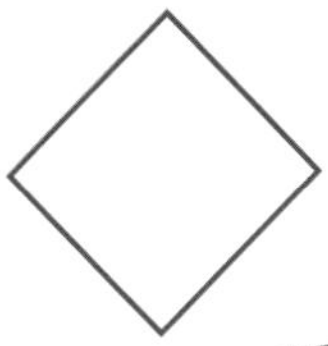

c

d

e

f

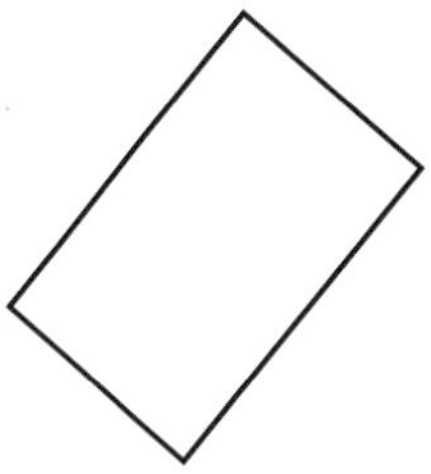

Triangles

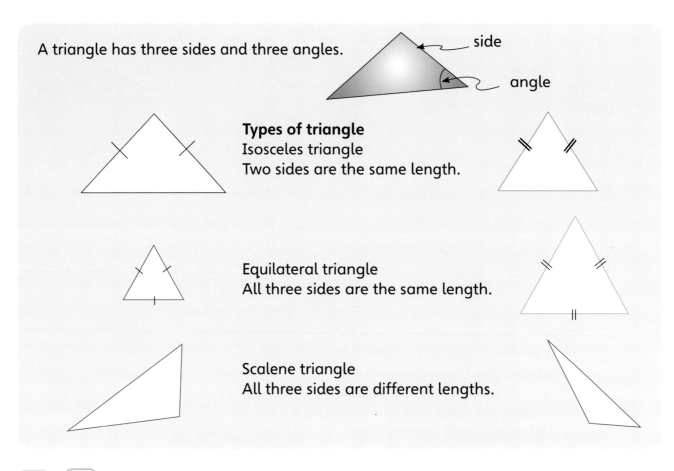

A triangle has three sides and three angles.

side

angle

Types of triangle
Isosceles triangle
Two sides are the same length.

Equilateral triangle
All three sides are the same length.

Scalene triangle
All three sides are different lengths.

A **1** Say whether each triangle is isosceles, equilateral or scalene.

a   b   c   d   e

2 Use the triangles above to help you copy and complete the statements below.
a   The smaller the angle, the _____ the length of the opposite side of the triangle.
b   The bigger the angle, the _____ the length of the opposite side of the triangle.

B What type of triangle is this?
How do you know?

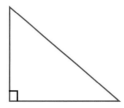

C Draw three different types of triangle: isosceles, equilateral and scalene. Colour each triangle with a different colour. Label your triangles. Write underneath each triangle what makes it isosceles, equilateral or scalene.

Quadrilaterals

A quadrilateral is any plane shape with four sides.

Can you name two types of quadrilateral?

A List which shapes are quadrilaterals.

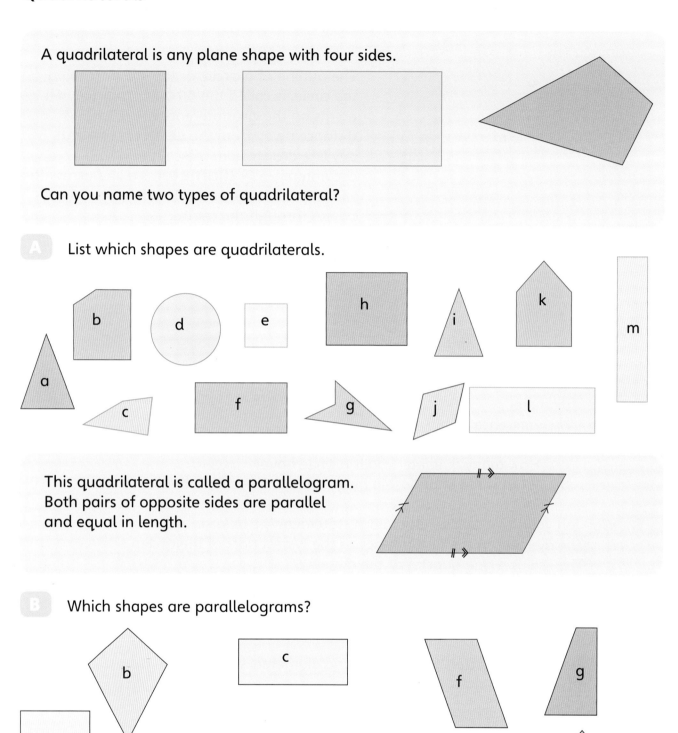

This quadrilateral is called a parallelogram.
Both pairs of opposite sides are parallel
and equal in length.

B Which shapes are parallelograms?

C Say whether each statement is true or false.
a All squares are parallelograms.
b All parallelograms are squares.
c A rectangle is a parallelogram.
d All parallelograms are rectangles.

Parts of a circle

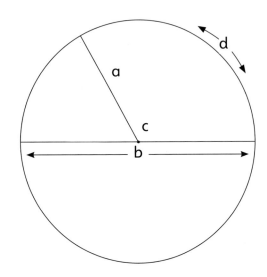

The outline of a circle, or the line describing the circle, is called the **circumference**. All points on the circumference are the same distance away from the **centre**. A **radius** is any line drawn from the centre to the circumference. A **diameter** is a line across the widest part of the circle. The diameter always passes through the centre.

A Work with a friend.

1. Identify each of the following parts on the circle above.
    a   radius
    b   centre
    c   diameter
    d   circumference

2. a   How many diameters does a circle have?
    b   What is the relationship between the radius and the diameter?

B Work on your own. Say whether each statement is true or false.
a   The diameter is the distance across the widest part of the circle.
b   The radius is one-quarter of the diameter.
c   The plural of radius is radii.
d   A circle has only 10 diameters.
e   All the points on the circumference are the same distance from the centre.

C a   Write down the letters for the radii and diameters shown in the diagram below.

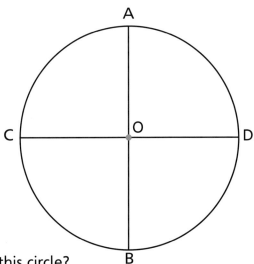

b   Where is the centre of this circle?

Circumference and diameter

A

1 Find a tin of milk which has a circular base. Measure the distance across the widest part of this circular base.

   a What is this distance called?

   b Copy this and fill in your measurement. d ____ = ____ cm

2 Use a piece of string to measure the distance around the can.

   a What is this distance called?

   b Copy this and fill in your measurement. c ____ = ____ cm

3 Now work out $\frac{\text{circumference}}{\text{diameter}}$.

B Repeat the last activity with four other tins of different sizes.

   a Is there a relationship between the circumference and the diameter of a circle?

   b What is this relationship?

$$\frac{\text{circumference}}{\text{diameter}} = \pi$$

$$= \text{approximately } \tfrac{22}{7} \text{ or } 3.14$$

$$\text{circumference} = \pi \times \text{diameter or } 2 \times \pi \times \text{radius}$$

C

1 Calculate the circumference of each of the following circles. (Use $\pi = 3.14$)

   a circle with diameter 5.5 cm

   b circle with diameter 8.2 cm

   c circle with radius 7 cm

   d circle with radius 3 cm

2 Calculate the diameter of each of the following circles.

   a circle with radius 9 cm

   b circle with radius 0.23 cm

   c circle with circumference 22 cm (Use $\tfrac{22}{7} = \pi$)

   d circle with circumference 88 km (Use $\tfrac{22}{7} = \pi$)

3 Calculate the radius of each of the following circles.

   a circle with diameter 10 km

   b circle with circumference 66 cm (Use $\tfrac{22}{7} = \pi$)

Why is it not practical to work with the actual value of π ?

Measuring circles

1 Use a ruler to help you measure the diameter of each circle.

a  b 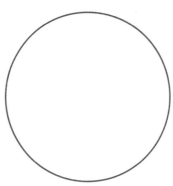 c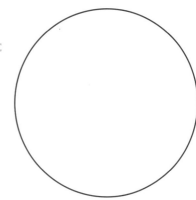

After you have measured the diameter, use the formula on page 79 to work out the circumference.

2 Find the circumference of the following circles. Use $\pi = \frac{22}{7}$.

a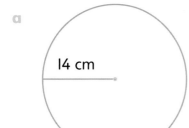
14 cm

b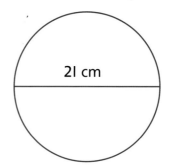
21 cm

3 Use a pair of compasses to help you draw the following circles.
a a circle with a radius of 2 cm
b a circle with a diameter of 5 cm
c a circle with a radius of 3.5 cm

B The diameter of a circular clock is 54 cm. How many centimetres does the hour hand travel in 1 hour? Use $\pi = 3.14$ to help you work this out.

C A cyclist rides around a circular field once. The radius of the field is 21 metres. How far does the cyclist ride if he goes around the field:
a once?
b three times?
   (Use $\pi = \frac{22}{7}$)

Symmetry

A **1** Trace and cut out the shapes below.

2 Which of the shapes would match exactly if you folded them along the dotted line?

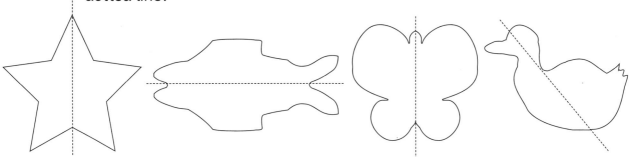

If a shape is folded in two parts and one part covers the other part exactly, the fold line is called a line, or axis of symmetry.

B **1** Trace these letters.
  a Which of them have lines of symmetry?
  b Draw in the lines of symmetry.

A B C D E F G H X Y

2 Trace these shapes.
  a How many lines of symmetry does each shape have?
  b Draw in the lines of symmetry.

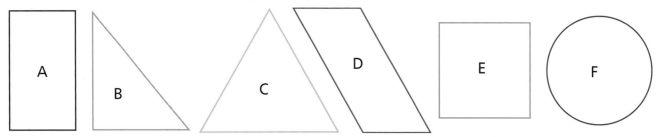

3 Trace these shapes. Which shapes do not have any lines of symmetry?

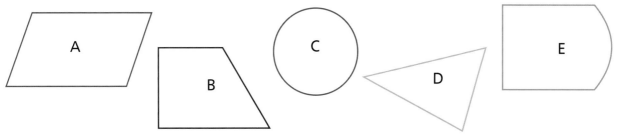

C Choose one of the shapes above to trace and cut out. Create three different patterns by repeating your shape in different ways: turning it; flipping it; sliding it along a line.

Congruence

When two shapes fit each other exactly, they are called congruent shapes. That means that their corresponding sides and angles are equal.

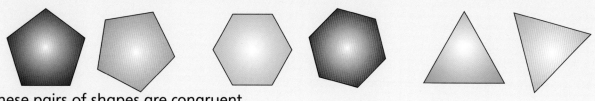

These pairs of shapes are congruent.

A **1** Identify which two shapes are congruent in each set.

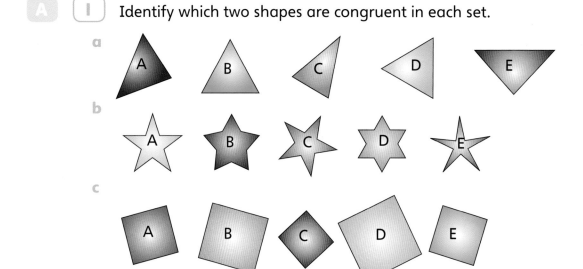

a

A B C D E

b

A B C D E

c

A B C D E

2 Work with a partner. Each draw three plane shapes. Exchange drawings. Draw three shapes that are congruent to your partner's shapes.

Sorting plane shapes

A Copy the table. Complete it by ticking the boxes that apply to each shape.

Shape	Edges	Curves	Right Angles	Parallel Lines	Lines of Symmetry
Rhombus					
Square					
Rectangle					
Right Angled Triangle					
Equilateral Triangle					
Scalene Triangle					

Isosceles Triangle					
Kite					
Trapezium					
Circle					
Parallelogram					

B Examine the shapes in the box carefully.

1 Decide how you could group these shapes. You can use properties such as number of sides, types of angles, parallel lines and lines of symmetry to make your groups.

2 Tell a partner how many groups you have made and what properties you used to place the shapes in each group.

C The boxes contain riddles that give information about various shapes. Read each riddle carefully and draw the shape(s) that corresponds to the riddle.

A
I am a four-sided closed figure with four lines of symmetry. My edges are parallel and perpendicular to each other. My diagonals bisect each other at right angles.

B
I have three equal sides. My interior angles each measure 60°. I contain three lines of symmetry.

C
I am a four-sided figure with two pairs of equal sides. I have one pair of equal angles and one line of symmetry.

D
I am a four-sided figure with opposites sides equal. My adjacent sides are perpendicular and I have 2 lines of symmetry. My diagonal bisects me to form two congruent triangles.

E
I am a three-sided polygon with one right angle. My longest side is called the hypotenuse. I am also an isosceles triangle.

F
I am a quadrilateral. I have one pair of parallel sides and no lines of symmetry.

Solids

A solid is an object that takes up space. Most solids have length, breadth and height. Some examples of solids are cubes, cones, prisms, spheres and cylinders. In this chapter, you will study the properties of some solids and learn how to make them using their nets.

A Name the different shapes and solids in this picture.

B **1** Mark and cut straight across an orange, as shown in the picture.

    a What kind of solid is an orange?

    b What is the shape of the cut surface?

    2 Name the shape of the surface when you cut each of these solids straight across.

    a a cone   **b** a cube

    c a cylinder (widthways)   **d** a cylinder (lengthways)

C Use straws, card, sticky tape and plasticine to make models of these shapes: cube, cuboid, sphere, cylinder, cone and pyramid. Examine them carefully, then copy and complete this table.

Shape	Number of faces	Number of vertices	Number of edges
cube			
cuboid			
cylinder			
cone			
pyramid			
sphere			

Nets of solids

If you open out a solid, a plane figure is formed.
The plane figure is called the net of a solid.

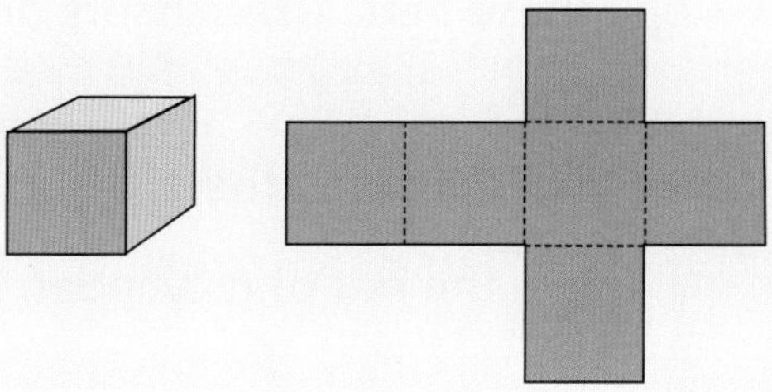

A Trace the following nets onto squared paper. Then cut out the nets along the solid lines, fold along the dotted lines and use tape to make the solid. Name the solids you have made.

a

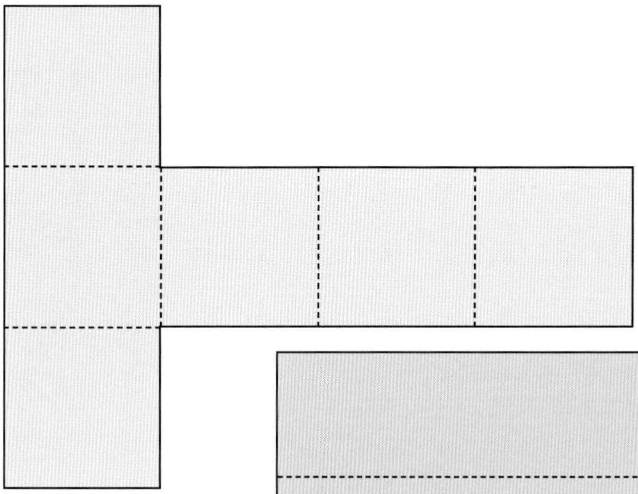

b

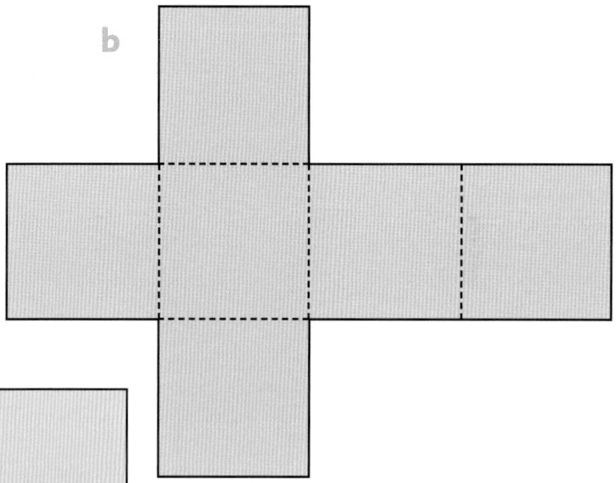

c

d

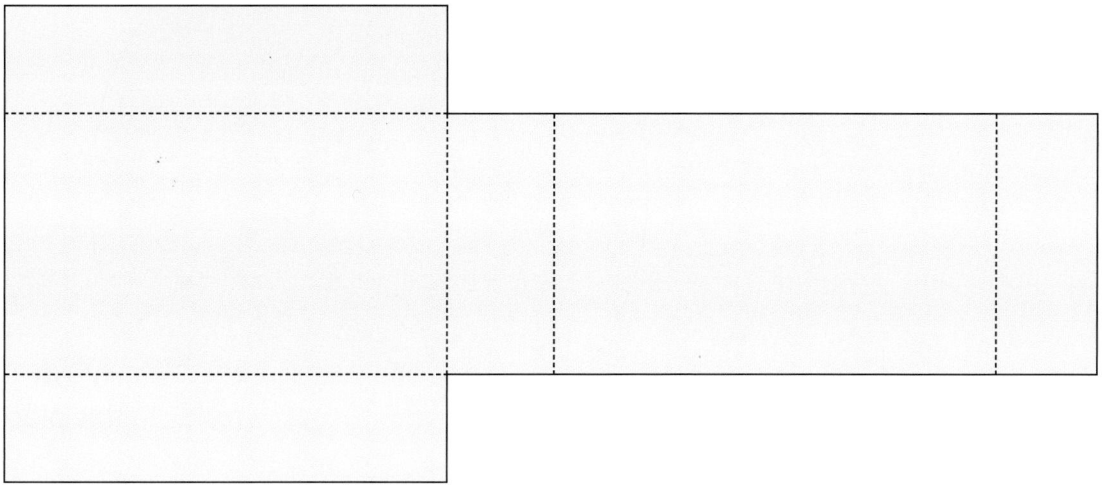

Cylinders and cones

A Copy these nets. Use scissors and tape to help you make the solid.

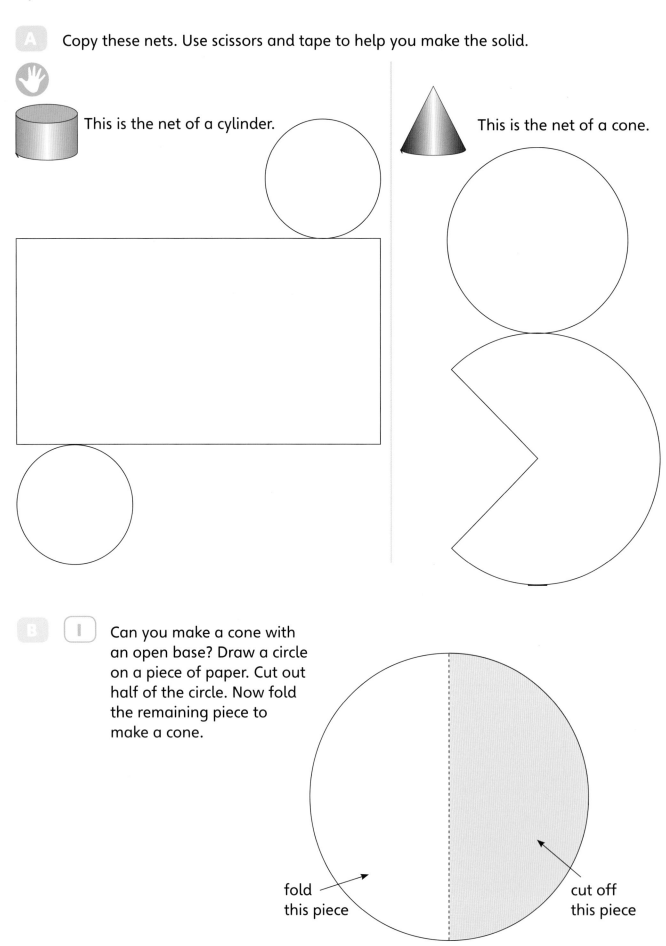

This is the net of a cylinder.

This is the net of a cone.

B **I** Can you make a cone with an open base? Draw a circle on a piece of paper. Cut out half of the circle. Now fold the remaining piece to make a cone.

fold
this piece

cut off
this piece

Pyramids and prisms

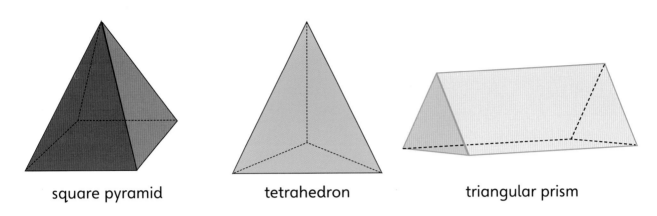

square pyramid   tetrahedron   triangular prism

A **1** Draw the following nets on squared paper.

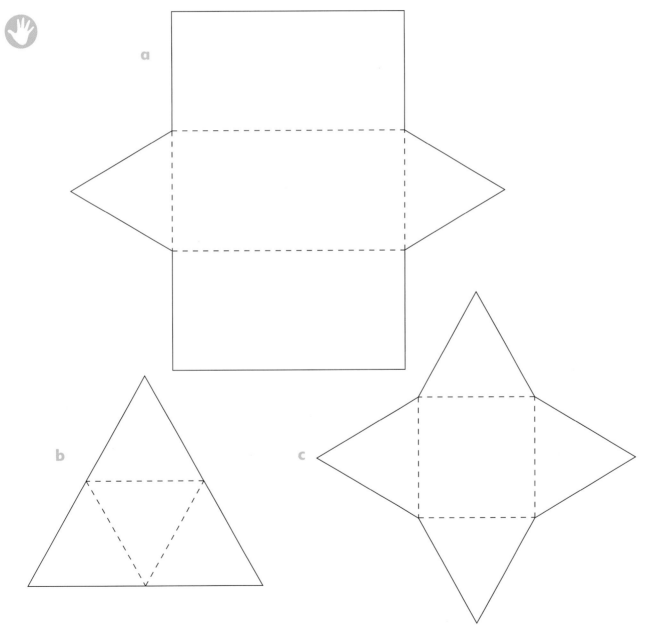

a

b

c

2 Now cut out the nets and make the solids. Name the solids you have made.

Sorting solids

A Write down the letter of the shape that is the odd one out in each group. Give a reason why this shape is the odd one out.

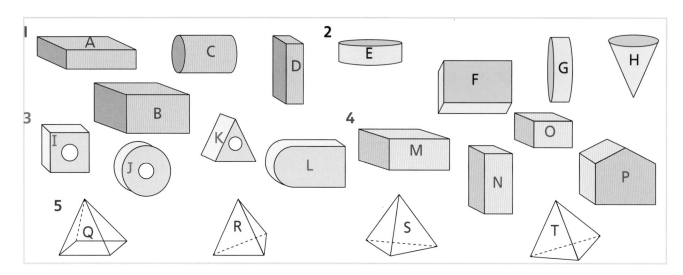

B Copy this table. Find at least five examples of each type of shape at school or home. Write the name of the object in the correct place in the table.

Cone	Cube	Cuboid	Cylinder	Pyramid	Sphere

Drawing solids

A Draw each pair of faces in your book. Join them to make a solid shape and write the name of each shape.

a

b

B Draw the shapes that you would get if you joined the following solid shapes together.
a cuboid and cuboid
b cone + cone
c cone + cylinder
d cuboid + triangular prism
e cube + square-based pyramid.

Assessment

A

1 Look at the diagrams.
   a Name each angle using letters.
   b Write down whether each angle is acute, right, obtuse, straight or reflex.
   c Use your protractor to measure the size of each angle.

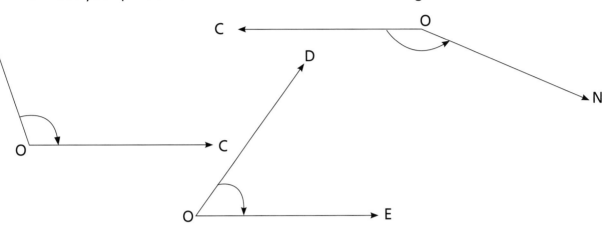

2 Use a ruler and protractor to construct the following angles.
   a 90°
   b 85°
   c 112°
   d 149°

B Copy and complete this table.

Shape	Number of vertices	Number of edges	Number of faces
Cube			
Cuboid			
Cone			
Cylinder			
Sphere			

C Which solid shapes have:
   a 6 edges
   b 6 vertices and 9 edges
   c no vertices

D Write the name of the shape that best describes the following objects:
   a A box of tissues
   b A tin of beans
   c A wooden plank
   d A telephone pole
   e An orange
   f The hole in a pencil sharpener
   g Dice

Assessment

 A Which of these nets could be folded to make a cube?

a 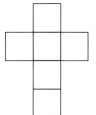 b  c 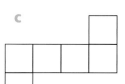 d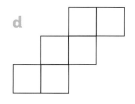

B This diagram is a tangram. The tangram was developed by the Chinese. It can be used to make many patterns. Trace the shapes and cut them out.

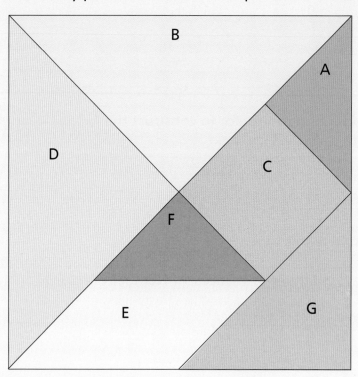

Draw each solution in the following activities.

1 Use the pieces to form these shapes.
  a a rectangle
  b an isosceles triangle
  c an equilateral triangle
  d a quadrilateral with one pair of parallel sides (trapezium)
  e a quadrilateral with two pairs of parallel sides (parallelogram)

For a special challenge, try to make each shape using all seven pieces!

2 Try to make these shapes.
  a a five-sided figure   b a six-sided figure

3 Make some other patterns of your own.

4 a How many times can shape F fit into shape B?
  b What fraction of the area of the tangram is shape E?
  c What fraction of the area of the tangram is shape G?

Measurement

We use a metric system of measurement to find out the length, mass or temperature of many things. In this chapter, you will learn about the metric units of length, mass and temperature. You will also work with scale drawings and convert units of measurement.

Length

Metric unit of length	kilometre	metre	centimetre	millimetre
Abbreviation	km	m	cm	mm

A **1** What is the most appropriate unit for measuring each item?

2 Measure these lengths, first to the nearest centimetre, and then in millimetres.

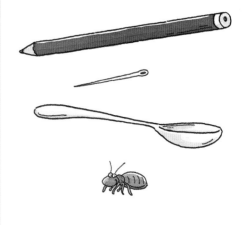

B Guess the lengths of each of these. Compare your guesses with those of a friend.
a the length of your longest finger
b the height of your classroom
c the distance from school to the nearest airport
d the height of the tallest tree in your street

C **1** Measure these lines in centimetres. Write your answers as a decimal.

a _____   b _____

c _____   d _____

2 If I cm represents 500 metres, what distance does each line in question I represent?

Scale drawing

A On this map, I cm represents 100 metres. Use your ruler to measure the distances. Give your answers in metres.

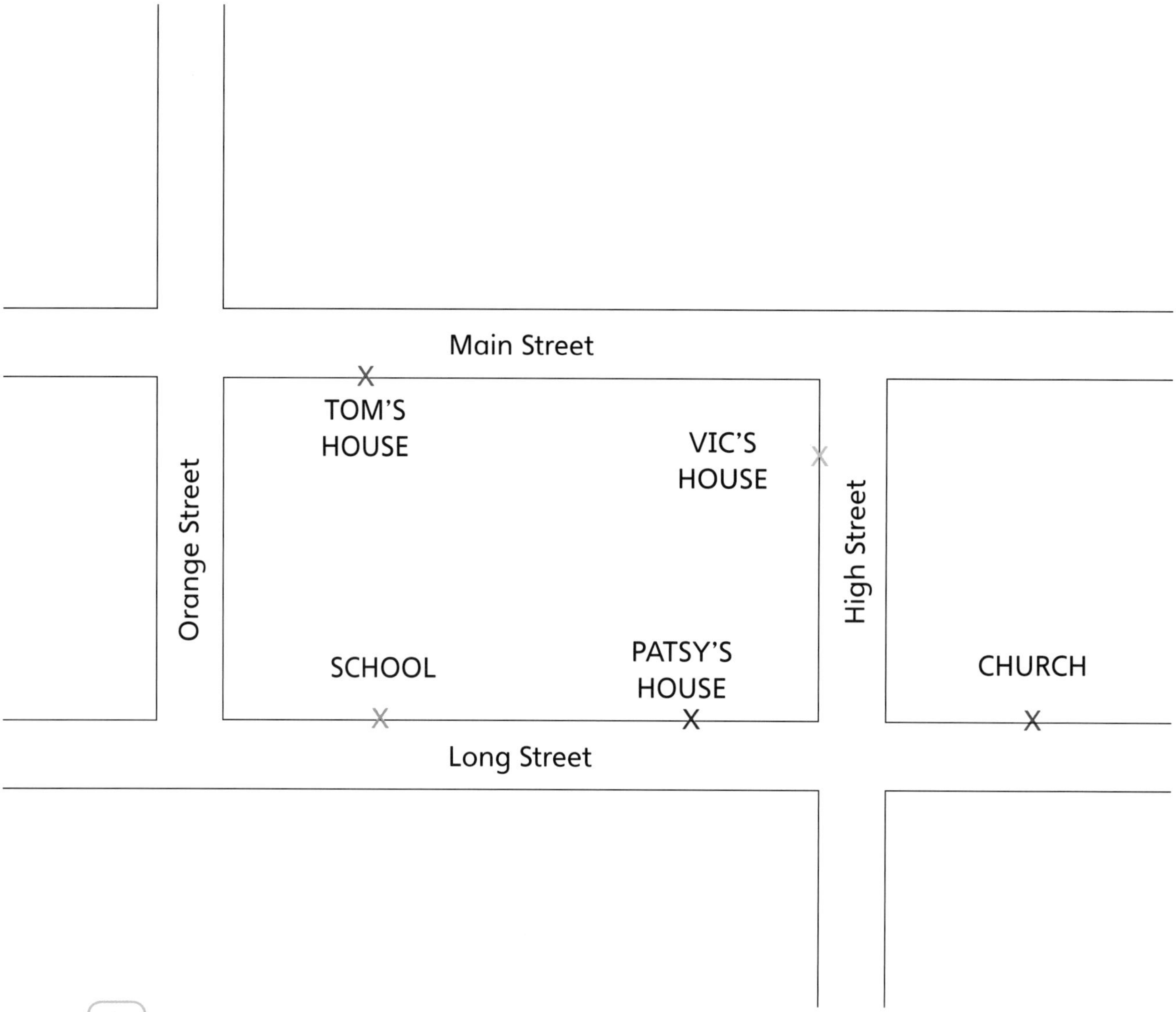

1 How far is it from:

a Tom's house to school?   b Vic's house to school?
c Patsy's house to school?   d Tom's house to Vic's house?
e Vic's house to church?   f Patsy's house to church?
g Patsy's house to Vic's house?   h Tom's house to church?

2 a What is the shortest route from Tom's house to Patsy's house?
b How far is this in metres?

Working with scale measurements

A This map shows the roads in a small town.

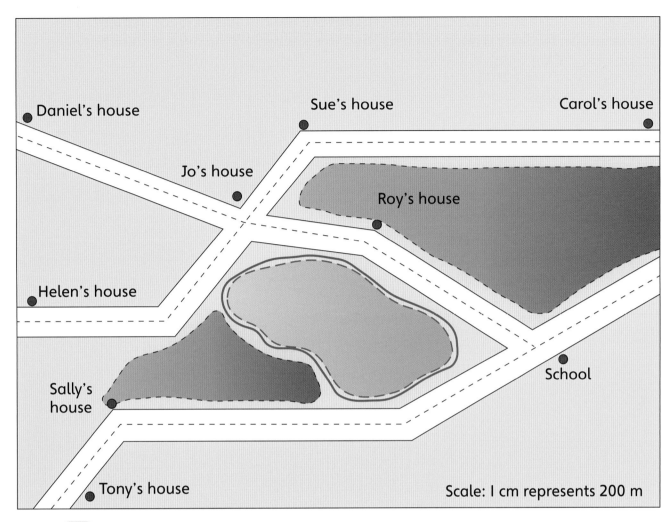

Daniel's house

Sue's house

Carol's house

Jo's house

Roy's house

Helen's house

Sally's house

School

Tony's house

Scale: I cm represents 200 m

1. Work out the following distances in metres. Measure along the roads.
   a from Carol's house to Tony's house   b from Sally's house to school
   c from Sally's house to Carol's house   d from Daniel's house to Tony's house
   e from Roy's house to Tony's house   f from Jo's house to school
   g from Helen's house to Daniel's house

2. Sue and Carol walk across the field to get to school.
   a How many metres does Sue walk?
   b How many metres does Carol walk?
   c If they walked along the road, how much longer would their route be?

B
1. On paper, I cm represents 5 km. If the actual distance between two towns is 40 km, what is the length on paper?
2. The actual distance between two islands is 96 km. If I cm on a map represents 6 km, what is the length on the map?
3. The actual distance between two towns is 55 km. If I cm on paper represents 10 km, what is the length on paper?
4. On a house plan, I cm represents 4 metres. If the length of the house is 30 metres, what is the length on the house plan?

Converting metric units of length

In the metric system, the metre is the standard unit of length. The metric system is based on decimal numbers. To convert between metric units of measurement, we multiply or divide by a power of ten. The table shows you the relationships between the main metric units of length.

		1 m	=	100 cm	=	1 000 mm
1 km	=	1 000 m	=	100 000 cm		
		0.01 m	=	1 cm	=	10 mm

A **1** Copy these and complete them.

a 1 km = _____ metres
b 1 metre = _____ cm
c 1 cm = _____ millimetres

2 Copy these and fill in the blanks.

a 51 m = _____ km   b 19 mm = _____ cm   c 0.08 cm = _____ mm

d 48.9 m = _____ cm   e 1.26 km = _____ m   f 7 cm = _____ m

B **1** Liz bought 3.84 metres of ribbon on Monday and 676 cm of ribbon on Tuesday. How many metres of ribbon did she buy altogether?

2 John walked 2.67 km. Henry walked 3 125 m.
a Who walked further?
b How much further did he walk? Give your answer in metres.

3 The length of my finger is 7.8 cm. What is the length of my finger in millimetres?

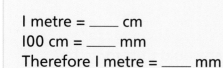

C Copy this and complete it.

I metre = _____ cm
100 cm = _____ mm
Therefore 1 metre = _____ mm

'Kilo' means 1 000, 'centi' means 100 and 'milli' means a thousandth.
Can you think of any other words that use these prefixes?
For example: century = 100 years.

Mass

Metric unit of mass	Abbreviation
Tonne	t
Kilogram	kg
Gram	g
Milligram	mg

A Copy the table and list five things which would be measured using each unit of measurement.

Tonne	Kilogram	Gram

B Select any eight objects which can be measured in kilograms or grams. Estimate the mass of each object. Then weigh each object to find out its actual mass. Draw a table like the one below and use it to record your findings.

Object	Estimated mass	Actual mass	Difference

C Judy went shopping. She brought home three bags of groceries. Calculate the total mass of the contents of each bag. Give your answers in kilograms.

a     550 g +    1.2 kg + 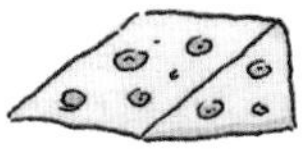   233 g

b 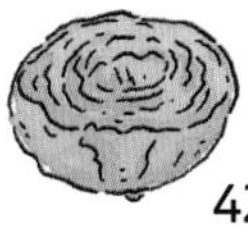 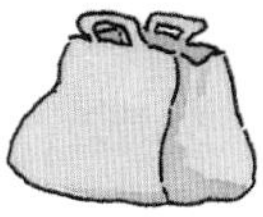   420 g + 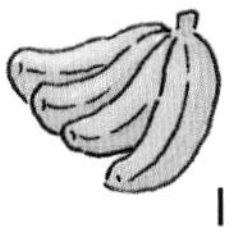 1.5 kg +  908 g

c 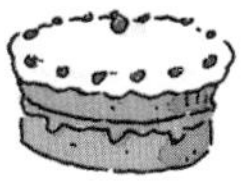    960 g + 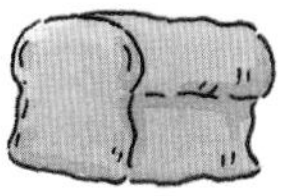 850 g +  500 g

More mass

I t = I 000 kg   I kg = I 000 g   I g = I 000 mg

A Copy these conversions and complete them.

a 420 g = ___ kg

b 1 518 mg = ___ g

c 1.22 t = ___ kg

d 3.7 kg = ___ t

e 0.4 g = ___ mg

f 0.08 kg = ___ g

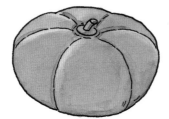

B ① A pumpkin weighs 2.4 kg. It is cut into five pieces of equal mass. Find the mass of each piece. Give your answer in grams.

② A truck weighs 3.18 tonnes. When carrying its load, the truck weighs 4.72 tonnes. Find the mass of the load in tonnes.

③ A potato weighs 400 grams. There are 42 potatoes in a box. If the empty box weighs 0.9 kg, what is the mass of the box of potatoes? Give your answer in kilograms.

④ A bag holds 56 kg of rice. A packet of rice holds 500 grams. How many packets of rice can be filled from the bag?

The dial in this picture shows a mass of 1.25 kg.

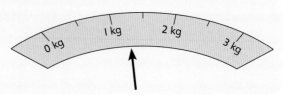

C Look at each scale and write down the mass it shows. Make sure to use the correct units of mass and write your answers as decimals.

a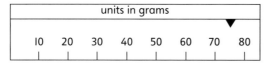

b

c

d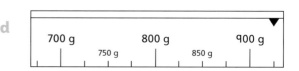

'Mass' and 'weight' have different meanings! Find out the difference between these words.
Explain why 'weight' is often used incorrectly in daily life.

Imperial and metric units

The measuring system we use today with metres, litres and kilograms is called the metric system. The metric system works in units of ten or powers of ten.

In the past, all Caribbean islands used a system of measurement called the imperial system of measurement. Some imperial measures are still used today. For example, you may have heard people use units such as gallons or quarts (for petrol and other liquids), feet and inches (for heights and small lengths), miles (for longer distances) and pounds and ounces (for mass).

Read the table carefully to find out how the metric units you know compare with imperial units.

Units of length	An inch is longer than a centimetre. One inch is approximately 2.5 cm (the length of the top part of your thumb) So, 5 cm is around 2 inches. A metre is longer than a foot. One metre is approximately three feet. Someone who is 1.5 metres tall is about 4 ½ foot tall. A six foot tall person is about 2 metres tall. A metre is about the same length as a yard (three feet). A mile is longer than a kilometre. There are about 1.6 kilometres in a mile.
Units of mass	A pound is lighter than a kilogram. There are just over 2 pounds in a kilogram (approximately 2.2 pounds). So, someone who weighs 50 kg will weigh over 100 pounds (approximately 110 pounds). An ounce is heavier than a gram. One ounce is approximately 30 grams.
Units of capacity	A pint is less than a litre. One litre is approximately 2 pints. A gallon is more than a litre. There are approximately 3.5 litres in a gallon.

A For each item, say what unit you would use to measure it in the metric system and which imperial unit could be used to measure the same thing.

a the mass of a person
b the amount of cool drink in a bottle
c the length of a door
d the distance from Jamaica to Trinidad
e the amount of gas in a car tank
f the amount of flour you need to bake a cake

B

1 Usain Bolt is almost 7 foot tall. What is this height (approximately) in metres?

2 Jess travels 4 miles to school and Pam travels 10 kilometres. Who travels the furthest?

3 Peter pays $6.20 for a gallon of petrol in Canada. His friend Doug pays $1.50 per litre in Barbados. Which petrol is more expensive?

4 A recipe calls for 12 ounces of dried fruit. Mrs Harrison has 200 grams of dried fruit. Does she have enough?

5 Rajah has a jug that holds 3 pints. About how many litres is this?

6 Theresa went on a diet and lost 5 kilograms. Her American friend asks her how much this is in pounds. What should Theresa say?

7 Measure the length of your pencil in centimetres. Approximately how many inches is this?

Temperature

What is temperature? What do you think is the temperature of each item shown in the pictures above?

A Copy this and complete it.

We use a _____ to measure temperature. The units of measurements for temperature are_____ . The hotter it is, the_____ the temperature. The colder it is, the_____ the temperature.

B Use the diagrams to help you answer the questions.
  a Which two scales are mainly used for measuring temperature?
  b What is the temperature of boiling water, in °F and °C?
  c What is the temperature of freezing water, in °F and °C?

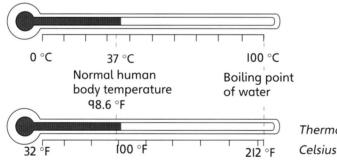

0 °C   37 °C   100 °C
              Normal human   Boiling point
              body temperature   of water
              98.6 °F

32 °F   100 °F   212 °F

Thermometers showing scales of Celsius and Fahrenheit

C

1 Listen to the weather report on radio or television for three days. Copy this table. Fill in the minimum and maximum temperatures for these three days.

Day	Minimum (in °C and °F)	Maximum (in °C and °F)

2 On Monday, during the day, the temperature in town was 10 °C. That night, the temperature dropped to –5 °C.
  a What was the difference between the daytime and night-time temperatures?
  b What was the overall average temperature on Monday (day and night)?
  c If the average temperature on Tuesday was 7 °C, what was the average temperature for Monday and Tuesday together?

Perimeter and area

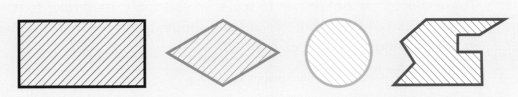

The thick line around each shape is the perimeter. The stripes show the area. In this chapter you will find the perimeter and area of regular, irregular and compound shapes, and solve real-life problems involving perimeter and area.

Perimeter is the distance around a shape. The perimeter is the sum of the lengths of all the sides of a shape. The perimeter of this shape is
12 cm + 3 cm + 12 cm + 3 cm = 30 cm

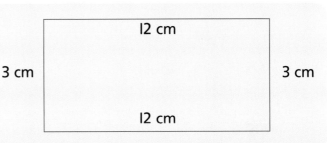

A Measure the perimeter of each shape in centimetres.

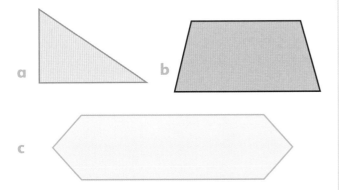

a

b

c

B Measure the sides of these shapes in millimetres and calculate each perimeter.

C **1** Harry ran around the edge of this field. How many metres did he run?

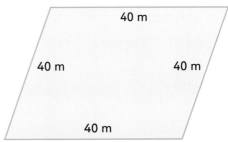

2 This church is built on an L-shaped piece of land. What is the perimeter of the land?

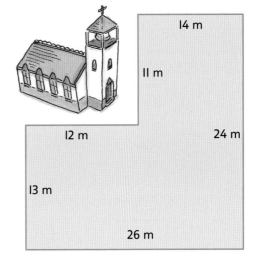

Finding perimeters

A **1** These shapes are not drawn to scale, so you can't use a ruler to measure them. Work out the perimeter of each shape, using the measurements given in the drawings.

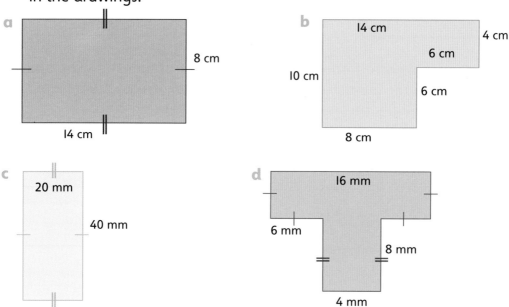

a   8 cm   14 cm

b   14 cm   4 cm   6 cm   10 cm   6 cm   8 cm

c   20 mm   40 mm

d   16 mm   6 mm   8 mm   4 mm

2 a   Find the perimeter of the triangle.

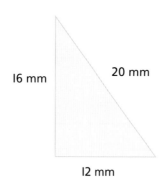

16 mm   20 mm   12 mm

b   One side of a square lawn measures 10 m. What is the perimeter of the lawn?

c   The width of a rectangular field is 8 m. Its length is twice the width. What is the perimeter of the field?

B **1** A rectangle measures 12 cm by 6 cm.

a   What is the perimeter of the rectangle?

b   If a square has the same perimeter as the rectangle, what is the length of one side?

2 The perimeter of a rectangle is 48 cm. If the width of the rectangle is 6 cm, what is the length?

C The length of rectangle A is 7.4 cm and the width is 4.8 cm. The perimeter of rectangle B is 14.9 cm. How much longer is the perimeter of rectangle A than the perimeter of rectangle B?

Working with perimeters

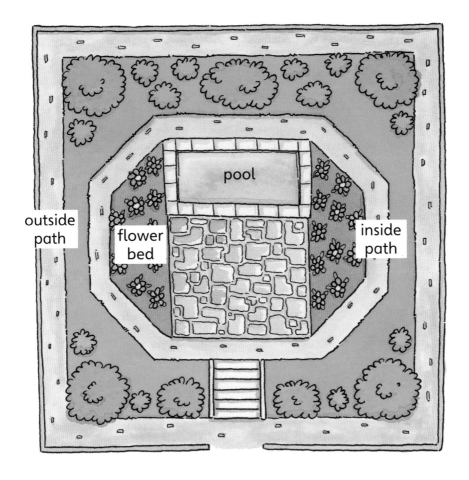

A Look at the bird's-eye view of the geometrically designed garden, and answer the questions below.

1   **a**   The whole garden is a square, with each side 50 m long. What is the perimeter of the garden?

     b   Janet walks three times around the outside path. How many metres does she walk?

     c   The length of Janet's step is 80 cm. How many steps does she take to walk around the outside path once?

2   An album is 20 cm long and 14 cm wide. Sal uses some lace to make an edge around the cover of the album. She has 12 cm left over afterwards. How long was her piece of lace?

3   The perimeter of a rectangular pool is 44 m. The length of the pool is 12 m.

     a   What is the width of the pool?

     b   If Janet wants to put a fence around two short sides and one long side of the pool, how many metres of fence does she need?

4   A rectangular table top has a length of 2.1 m and a width of 1.3 m.

     a   What is the perimeter of the table top?

     b   If Mark puts two of these tables next to each other, with the short sides touching, what is the combined perimeter of the table tops?

Areas of squares and rectangles

Area is the measure of the extent of a shape's surface. We measure area in square units.
For example:

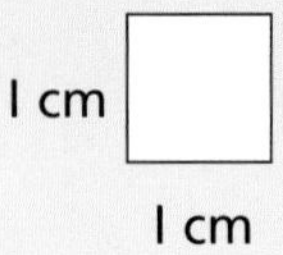

I cm [ ] = I square centimetre or I cm²
I cm

To calculate the area of a rectangle, we multiply length by breadth.
For example:

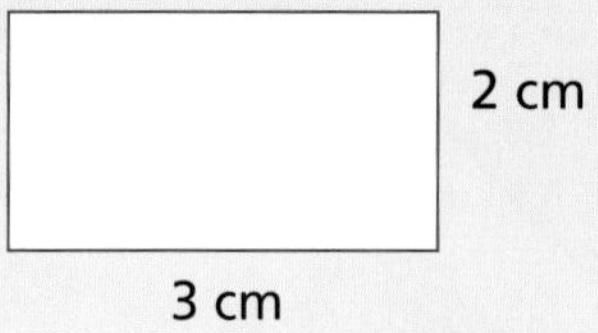

3 cm × 2 cm = 6 cm²
2 cm   The area of the rectangle is 6 cm².
3 cm

length
breadth (width)

Copy this and complete it.

The area of a rectangle = ____ × ____.

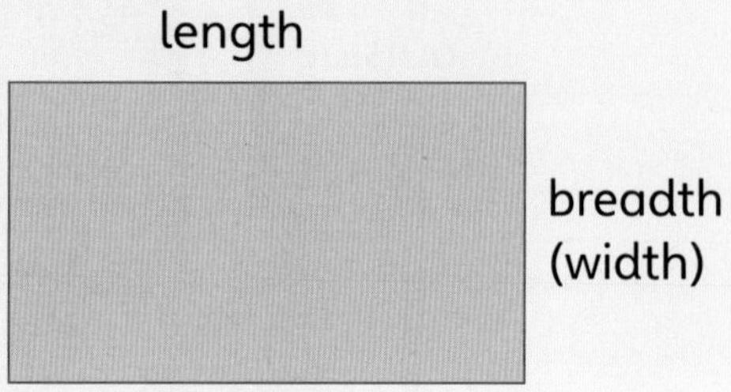

A ① Trace these rectangles. Place them on centimetre-squared paper.

a 
b
c

② Copy and complete this table for the rectangles in question I.

	Length	Width	Length × width	Area
a				
b				
c				

B ① Find the areas of these rectangles.

a
5 cm
3 cm

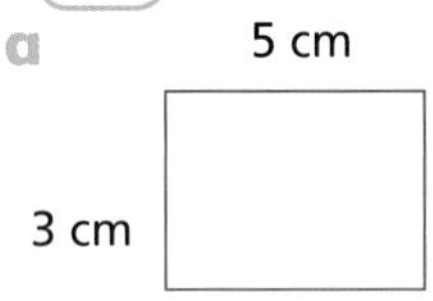

b
9 cm
4 cm

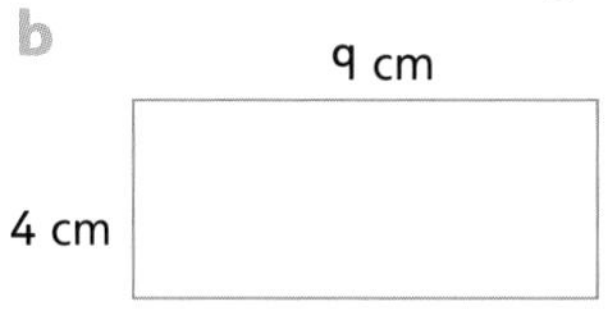

c
12 cm
3 cm

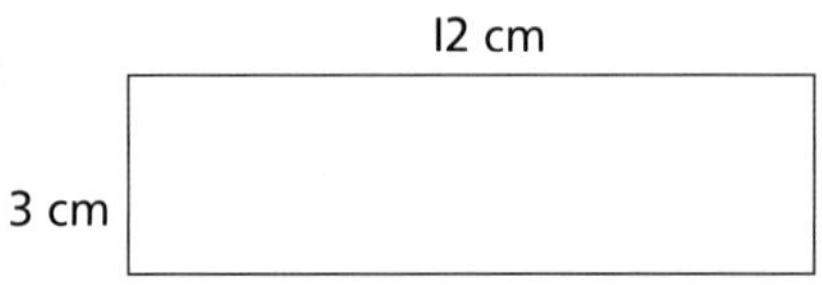

② Find the area of each rectangle.
a length 6 cm, width 4 cm
b length 9.2 cm, width 6 cm
c length 8.5 cm, width 7.3 cm

③ What is the area of a rectangle that measures 9 cm by 81 mm?

④ Copy and complete the following for each rectangle.
a area = 12 cm², width = 6 cm, length = ____
b area = 23.2 cm², length = 8 cm, width = ____
c area = 39 cm², width = ____, length = 6 cm
d area = 42 cm², length = ____, width = 60 mm

Solving problems involving perimeter and area

A Find the area of each rectangle.

a

```
          7 cm



                        4 cm


```

b

```
              6 cm


                      3 cm

```

B **1** If the length of a rectangular floor is 4 metres and the area is 31 m², what is the width?

2 The area of a rectangle is 120 cm². The width is 10 cm.
 a Find the length.
 b Find the perimeter.

3 The two lengths of a rectangle together measure 20 cm. The width is 8 cm. What is the area of the rectangle?

4 The length of a patch of land is twice its width. The width is 6 metres. What is the area of the land?

C **1** The width of this rectangle is half its length. The length is 19 m.
 a What is the perimeter of the rectangle?
 b What is the area of the rectangle?

19 m

```
┌──────────────────────────┐
│                          │
│                          │
│                          │
│                          │
│                          │
│                          │
└──────────────────────────┘
```

2 This is the floor plan of a room. It has been drawn so that 1 cm represents 6 m in the actual room.

```
┌──────────┐
│          │
│          │
└──────────┘
```

Find:
 a the length of the room
 b the width of the room
 c the area of the floor

Solving problems involving areas of squares

Copy this and complete it. The area of a square = ____ × ____.

A **1** Calculate the area of the following squares.

a
3 cm

3 cm

b
10 m

c
6.5 cm

d
10.7 cm

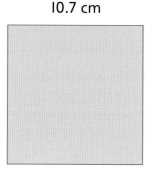

B **1** A square plot is 14 metres long. Find its area.

2
a Find its area in millimetres.

The side of a square discount stamp is 4.1 cm.

b A sheet of discount stamps has six rows of
stamps, with five stamps in a row. Find the
area of a sheet of discount stamps if there
are no spaces between the stamps.

c Find the area of the remaining sheet if one
row has been torn off.

C **1** A rug covers a square floor exactly. The length of a side of the floor is 8.2
metres. Calculate the area of the rug in square metres.

2 Find the area of a square whose sides each measure 5 cm.

104 Perimeter and area

More problems involving areas of squares

A

1. The area of a square is 81 mm². What is the length of one side?

2. The length of one side of a square is 5 cm. Find the perimeter and the area.

3. The perimeter of a square lawn is 120 m. Find its area.

B Mr Martin had 200 m of fencing wire. He used all of it to fence a square garden.
a. What is the length of one side of the garden?
b. What is the area of the garden?

C A piece of rope 64 cm long is formed into a square.
a. Find the length of a side of the square.
b. Find the area of the square.

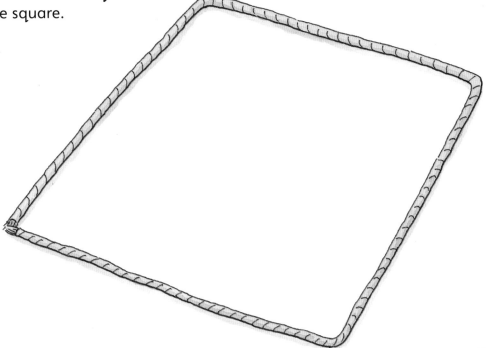

Area of triangles

A triangle is a shape that has only three straight sides and three interior angles. There is a special formula for working out the area of a triangle. Look at the grid. What is the area of rectangle ABCD?

Length = 4 cm, width = 3 cm

Area = 4 cm × 3 cm = 12 cm²

The triangle BCD takes up half the space of the rectangle.

$\frac{1}{2} \times$ (3 cm × 4 cm) = $\frac{1}{2} \times$ 12 cm²

= 6 cm²

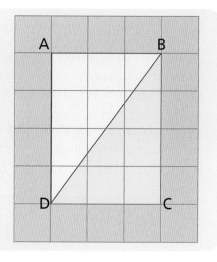

A For each of the following, use your ruler to measure the sides. Find the area of the rectangle, the area of half the rectangle, and the area of the shaded triangle.

a 　　b 　　c 　　d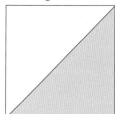

B Find the area of the triangles.

a
40 mm
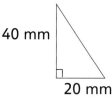
20 mm

b
4 cm
5 cm

c
3 cm　　4 cm
5 cm

C Find the area of the following shapes.

a
12 cm
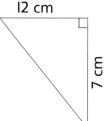
7 cm

b
8.2 cm
3.4 cm

c
9 cm
9 cm
15.6 cm

Can you write a rule for finding the area of a triangle?

Areas of compound shapes

Area is the amount of space taken up by a plane shape. You already know how to work out the area of a square and the area of a rectangle.

Area of a square = side × side

Area of a rectangle = length × width

Compound shapes are shapes made up of other shapes. You can work out the area of a compound shape by adding together the areas of the shapes it is made of.

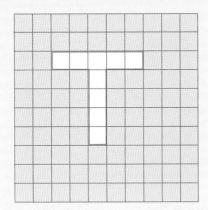 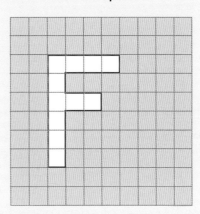

Count the squares to work out the area of each shape.

A Work out the area of each unshaded shape. Count the centimetre squares (cm²).

a

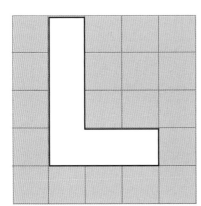

b

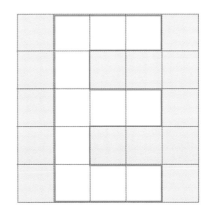

B Calculate the area of each shape. Divide them into squares or rectangles to make it easier.

a   b   c   d

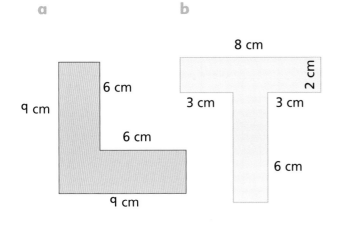 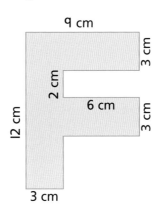 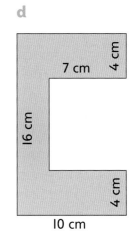

Solving problems using area

Look at this shape. It does not have a regular shape like a square, rectangle or triangle. How can we find the area of this irregular shape?

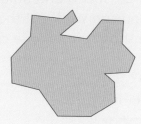

We can use the blocks to help us estimate the area of the shape. Each block = 1 cm².

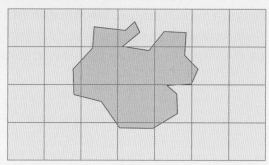

Count all the blocks covered by the shape. For all the blocks partly covered, estimate what fraction of the block is covered (for example, $\frac{5}{6}$ or $\frac{1}{10}$). Add all the fractions and whole numbers together and estimate the area.

A Estimate the area of each shaded shape by counting the covered squares and fractions of squares.

a

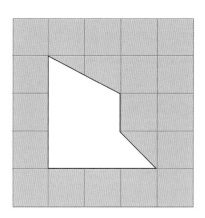

b

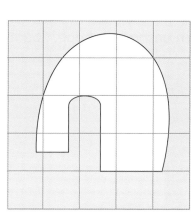

c

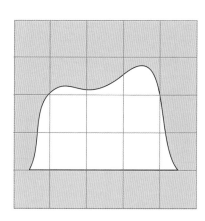

B On a piece of paper, draw the perimeter of your friend's hand and your own hand. On another piece, draw the perimeter of your friend's foot and your own foot. Estimate the areas and compare. Whose hand and foot takes up a larger area?

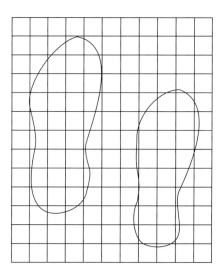

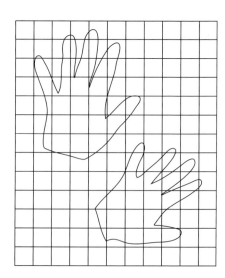

Time

We count time in seconds, minutes and hours. For longer periods of time, we count in days, weeks, months and years. In this chapter you will tell the time on different kinds of clocks, write the notation correctly and calculate durations and finishing times. You will also solve real-life problems involving distance, speed and time.

A What is the time:

a 35 minutes after 11:45 am?

b half an hour before 12 noon?

c 1 hour after midnight?

d 3 hours after 10 am?

e 20 minutes after 6:45 pm?

f 25 minutes after 11:35 am?

B 1 This is part of a flight schedule.

Flight number	From	Time due	Actual arrival
704	New York	6:05 pm	6:20 pm
501	Barbados	7:00 pm	7:00 pm
463	Trinidad	10:05 pm	9:45 pm

a Sue's aunt was arriving on flight 704 from New York. How many minutes late was the flight?

b Was the flight from Trinidad late or early, and by how many minutes?

c A plane due at 11:20 pm was 50 minutes late. At what time did it arrive?

2 An aeroplane leaves St Lucia at 6:30 am. The flying time to Martinique is 15 minutes. At what time is it expected to land?

C 1 What is:

a half an hour after 4:00 pm?

b 10 minutes before 3:00 pm?

c 9 days after Sunday?

d 11 days before Tuesday?

2 Copy and complete this table.

Time in words	This is the same as	Time in symbols
quarter to six	45 minutes past 5 or 15 minutes to 6	5:45
quarter to three		
	40 minutes past 10	
		8:35
ten to seven		

3 Draw clock faces to show these times.

a fifteen minutes past two

b 6:45

c half past three

d ten to five

e 1:25

The 24-hour clock

A 24-hour clock has numbers from 00 to 23 to show the times from midnight through to the following midnight. In the diagram, the am times are shown on the inner clock. The pm times are shown on the outer clock.

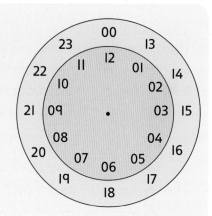

1:00 am is 1 hour after midnight and is written as 01:00
2:30 am is 2 hours and 30 minutes after midnight and is written as 02:30
12:30 am is half an hour after midnight and is written as 00:30
1:00 pm is 13 hours and is written as 13:00
2:30 pm is 14 hours and 30 minutes and is written as 14:30
10:15 pm is 22 hours and 15 minutes and is written as 22:15

A Complete the table.

	Time	24-hour clock
a	4:00 am	04:00
b	7:25 am	
c		03:05
d		07:15
e	11:45 am	
f	12:00 noon	

2 Write these 24-hour clock times using am.

a 08:18
b 06:20
c 01:30

B 1 Complete the table.

	Time	24-hour clock
a	6:00 pm	18:00
b	7:30 pm	
c	10:15 pm	
d		21:30
e	11:45 pm	
f	12:00 midnight	

2 Write these 24-hour clock times using pm.

a 14:00
b 23:35
c 18:15

3 Look at the airline timetable. It shows the times that four planes leave Toronto and arrive in Antigua.

Flight	Leaves Toronto	Arrives Antigua
CPM-1	10:05	16:30
CPM-2	14:15	21:50
CPM-3	15:30	23:20
CPM-4	16:45	22:40

a Which is the fastest flight?
b Which is the slowest flight?
c Make another timetable showing these times, using am and pm.

Working with time

A

1. Lucy was born on 1 December 2001. How old will she be on 1 December 2009?

2. In 2007, Lucy's dad turned 40. In what year was he born?

3. In 1991, Danny turned 6.
   a. In what year was he born?   b. How old will he be in 2025?

4. Jonathan was 16 years old in 2008. In that year, his brother was half his age and his mother was five times his brother's age.
   a. How old was their mother in 2008?   b. In what year was she born?

5. In 1998, Jonathan's grandfather was 56 years old. In what year was he born?

B Look at each of the gravestones.

1. Work out in which year each person was born.

2. Work out how old they would have been if they were still alive now.

Elijah Worryfellow died August 1922 age 67 "No more worries, old fellow!"

Agnes Singlethread passed on in the winter of 1878 at the ripe old age of 92 "May you weave with the angels, dearest"

Johnny Cod lost to the seas in 1902 aged 17 R.I.P.

Sarita Beanie died of sudden illness in 1935 at the tender age of 11 Missed sadly

C

1. a. Which month has only three letters in its name?
   b. Which month has the most letters in its name?
   c. How many days are there from 7 April to 7 May?
   d. How many days were there from 20 February to 18 March 2000?
   e. How many weeks and days are there from 1 March to 30 April?

2. Mrs Singh was on a course from 1 April to 19 August. How many days did the course last?

Assessment

A **1** A bus left a village at 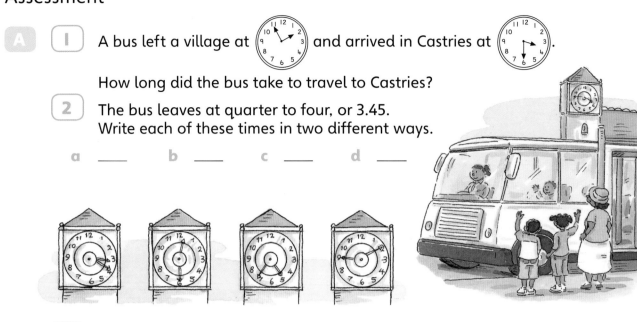 and arrived in Castries at .

How long did the bus take to travel to Castries?

2 The bus leaves at quarter to four, or 3.45.
Write each of these times in two different ways.

a ____   b ____   c ____   d ____

3 The bus driver works eight hours each day of a five-day week. How many hours does she work in four weeks?

B **1** A bus makes 1 020 trips per year. If it makes the same number of trips each month, how many trips does it make per month?

2 A bus transports 34 passengers every day. The bus runs five days a week. How many passengers does it transport in two weeks?

3 A bus arrives at 35-minute intervals. The last bus left at 13:15. Write the arrival times of the next six buses.

C Copy the column and fill in the correct words to match each definition.

100 years	
1 000 years	
every 24 hours	
ten years	
every 12 months	
two weeks	
seven days	
12 times a year	

daily   week   monthly   fortnight   century   decade   annual   millennium

E-mail dates and times

A This is Ella's inbox. Use the information on the screen to help you answer the questions.

Ella's Inbox

From	Subject	Sent
Mike Mc Gee	Holidays!	09/04/2009
Jenny Press	Re: Information on cats	04/04/2009
Dan Simmonds	Making fudge	04/04/2009
The Cat Site	Re: Cats	03/04/2009
----------	Re: Cats	29/03/2009
Mike Mc Gee	Jokes	28/03/2009
Kitties and Puppies Co	Re: Cats	28/03/2009
Big Cats Online	Re: Cats	28/03/2009
Sylvie Johnson	Cool website	25/03/2009
Doris Phillips	Choir practice cancelled	18/03/2009
Angela Mc Gee	Mike's e-mail address	15/03/2009
Sylvie Johnson	Jokes	03/03/2009
Dan Simmonds	Guess what?!!	27/02/2009

1 a In which year did Ella receive these emails?
   b In which months did she receive them?

2 a In which of the months did Ella receive the most emails?
   b In which of the months did Ella receive the least emails?

3 Ella was doing a project about cats. On which dates did she receive responses to her enquiries about cats?

4 This symbol means the message had an attachment ✐. On which dates did Ella receive messages with attachments?

5 Which two emails arrived exactly a month apart?

6 a Who sent Ella an email in the last week of February?
   b How many days passed before the next email from the same person?

Distance, speed and time

When we travel, we often need to work out the speed at which we are travelling. Speed tells us how much time it takes to cover a given distance.

Average speed $= \dfrac{\text{Distance}}{\text{Time}}$

For example:

Lisa cycled 8 kilometres in 2 hours. What was her average speed?

Speed $= \dfrac{8 \text{ km}}{2 \text{ hours}}$

$= 4 \text{ km/h}$

Her average speed was 4 km/h.

We can use this rule to work out distance travelled, using average speed and time.

Distance = Average speed × Time

Or we can work out the time taken to travel, using average speed and distance.

Time $= \dfrac{\text{Distance}}{\text{Average speed}}$

A

1 A car travels 240 km at an average speed of 50 km/h. How long does the trip take?

2 Mr Brown drove his car at an average speed of 80 km/h. How many kilometres did he travel in:

   a 4 hours   b $5\frac{1}{2}$ hours   c $2\frac{1}{4}$ hours

3 Copy and complete the table.

Average speed	Distance	Time
40 km/h	80 km	
36 km/h		$1\frac{1}{2}$ hours
	64 km	1 hour 20 minutes

B These are the finishing times for a cycle race. The distance of the race was 120 km. Find:

a Simone's average speed.

b Jamie's average speed.

c Ellen's average speed.

d Milly rode the race at an average speed of 50 km/h. How long did she take to finish?

Doogie takes the cup for the Smiley Lollipops Cycle Race!

Simone Doogie once again won the Smiley Lollipops Cycle Race. She finished the race in exactly $1\frac{1}{2}$ hours. Jamie Wallace took second place, finishing in 1 hour and 40 minutes, and Ellen Bryce took third place, finishing in 1 hour and 48 minutes.

Assessment

A **1** Find the area of each shape shown in the grid below. Each square is 1 cm².

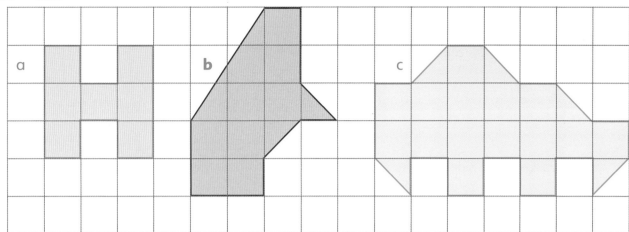

2 Copy and complete these sentences about the shape FGHJ.

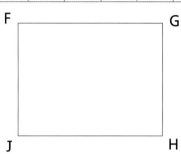

a   The length FG is _____ cm.
b   The width is _____ cm.
c   The perimeter of the figure is _____ cm.
d   The area is _____ cm².
e   Copy the figure and draw in a diagonal. The length of the diagonal is _____ cm.
f   The diagonal divides the figure into halves. Shade half the figure. The shaded part has three sides. It is a _____ .
g   The area of the shaded part is _____ cm².

B **1** Rewrite as grams, using decimals.
a   119 mg = _____ g   b   3 759 mg = _____ g   c   1 295 mg = _____ g

2 Convert these measurements to metres.
a   530 cm   b   95 cm   c   756 cm   d   2 cm   e   4 184 cm

3 Measure each line. Give your answers in centimetres and in millimetres.
a   _____
b   _____
c   _____
d   _____

C **1** The sides of a triangle measure 1.75 cm, 2.5 cm and 3.08 cm.
What is the perimeter of the triangle?

Assessment

A **1** Calculate the area of the shaded shapes . Give your answers in cm².

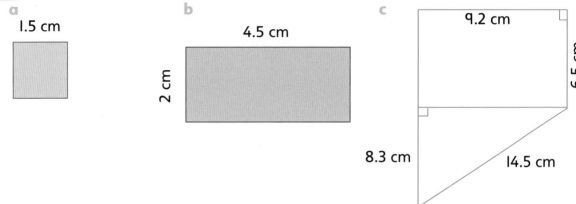

a 1.5 cm

b 4.5 cm 2 cm

c 9.2 cm 6.5 cm 8.3 cm 14.5 cm

2 The area of a rectangular table cloth is 1.2 m². Its length is 150 cm. What is its width?

3 Measure the sides of each triangle. Then calculate the perimeter of each triangle.

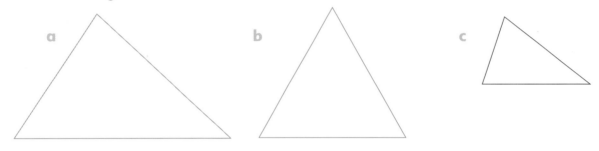

a   b   c

B **1** Choose the correct answers from the brackets to complete these sentences.
a Quarter to five is also written (5:15, 4:45, 5:00, 4:15).
b Half an hour after 4:30 pm is (05:30, 04:15, 04:35, 16:00, 17:00).
c Ten minutes before 10:00 am is (10:10 am, 10:10 pm, 9:50 am, 9:55 am; 9:10 am).
d From 14 April to 20 April, there are (5 days, 6 days, 7 days, 8 days, 9 days).

2 Write the following times as you would find them on a 24-hour clock.
a half past three in the afternoon   b   twenty to one in the afternoon
c five to eight in the evening   d   five minutes before midnight

C **1** A car driving at a steady speed travels 60 km in three hours. How many kilometres will it travel at the same speed in eight hours?

2 The distance between Georgetown and Rosignol is shown on a map by a line 5.4 cm long. The scale on the map is 1 cm = 12 km. Work out the actual distance between the two places.

3 A floor is 9 m long and 12 m wide. How many square tiles with side 30 cm will completely cover the floor?

Volume and capacity

In this chapter you will estimate, measure and record the capacity and volume of various objects. You will also convert between units of measurement for volume and capacity, and solve real-life problems involving volume and capacity.

The volume of a solid is the amount of space it occupies.

A   Use centimetre cubes to make these solids. Then find the volume of each in cubic centimetres.

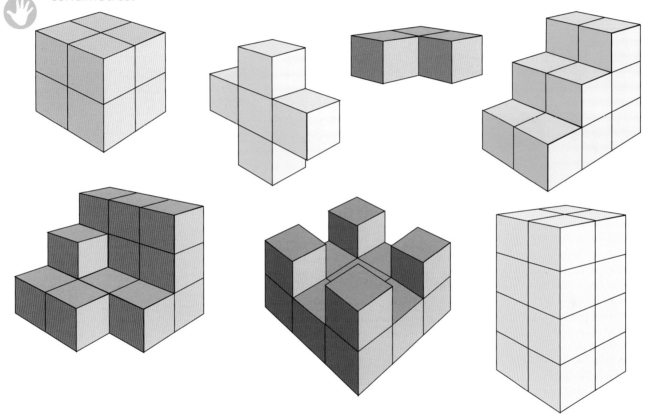

B   Draw diagrams to show these problems, and then find the answers. You could also use cubes to help you.

1   **a**   In a box of milk, six tins can fit in one row, and the box can take four rows. How many tins can fit in one layer in the box?

   b   If the box can hold three layers of tins, how many tins can the box hold?

2   A crate of sardines contains a hundred tins. Four tins fit along the width of the crate and five tins fit along the length. How many layers of tins are in the crate?

3   A carton of soap powder holds two boxes along its height and four boxes along its width. There are 48 boxes in the carton. How many boxes fit along the length of the carton?

4   A toy box holds 36 building bricks. The bricks are packed in four layers, with three bricks along its length. How many bricks fit along the width of the box?

Volume

We measure volume in cubic units. A cubic centimetre is written cm^3, and a cubic metre is written m^3.
We calculate the volume of a cube or cuboid using the following formula:
Volume = length × breadth × height

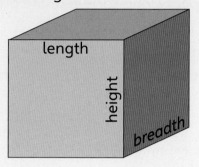

A **1** Find the volume of the following cubes.

a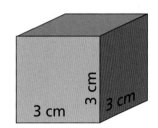

b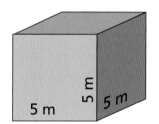

2 Find the volume of the following cuboids.

a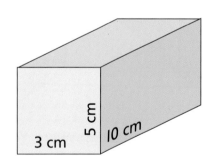

b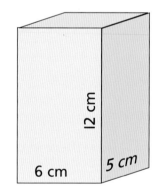

B **1** A rectangular box is 8 cm long, 6 cm wide and 3 cm high. What is the volume of the box?

2 The volume of a box is 162 cm^3. If the length is 9 cm and the width is 6 cm, what is the height of the box?

3 The volume of a cube is 2 cm^3. How many of these cubes can fit into a box that is 8 cm long, 5 cm wide and 4 cm high?

4 The volume of a tank is 2 160 cm^3. The length is 15 cm. If the width and the height are equal measurements, what is the width?

Working with metric units of capacity

Capacity is the amount that something can hold when it is full. Look at these cups. Which do you think holds the most?

I litre = I 000 millilitres
I litre = I 000 ml
So I 027 ml can be written as I litre 27 ml or $1\frac{27}{1\,000}$ litres or 1.027 litres.

A

1 Name four objects whose capacity can be measured in litres.

2 Would you measure the capacity of these in litres or millilitres?

a   b   c   d   e

3 Write these in litres, using decimals.

a 125 ml	b 15 ml	c 2.5 ml	d 306 ml	e 2 498 ml
f 51.39 ml	g 31 000 ml	h 216.8 ml	i 6 ml	

4 Convert to millilitres.

a 1.960 l	b 3.006 l	c 16 l	d 2.4 l
e 0.67 l	f 81 l	g 0.057 l	h 0.3 l

B

 The volume of this cube is I cubic centimetre (I cm³). If water fills a cubic centimetre of space, we say the cube has a capacity of I millilitre (I ml). The volume of this box is 8 cm³. The box has a capacity of 8 ml.

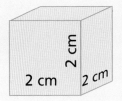

 Go to a local store and find ten things whose capacity is measured in millilitres and ten things whose capacity is measured in litres. Make a list of what you find out.

Working with capacity

The capacity of a container is the amount it can hold when it is full. A container whose volume is 1 000 cm³ has a capacity of 1 litre.

A

1. A large jar holds 3 l of water when full. What is the volume of the jar?

2. The volume of a bucket is 3 500 cm³. How many litres of water will fill the bucket?

3. The volume of a tank is 28 500 cm³. 24 litres of water are poured into the tank. How many more litres of water are needed to fill the tank?

4. A box is 28 cm long, 16 cm wide and 10 cm deep. Find the capacity of the box in litres.

5. A container holds 2.4 l of water when full.
   a What is the volume of the container?
   b The volume of a cup is 15 cm³. How many cups of water can be filled from the container?

B

1. Copy this and complete it.
   1 l = _____ cm³
   1 l = _____ ml
   1 ml = _____ cm³

2. The volume of a bottle of medicine is 150 cm³. Jenny must take a teaspoonful of the medicine every day. If one teaspoon holds 5 ml of liquid, in how many days will the medicine be finished?

C For each photograph, write down the amount of liquid contained in the jug in ml and cm³.

a

b

c

d

Collecting and representing data

Another name for information is data. We can find out data from many sources – from listening to our friends, families and teachers, from our own observations, and from the media. In this chapter you will collect data using a variety of methods including observation, interviews and questionnaires. You will represent data in different ways, and read and interpret data from various graphs, charts and tables.

Simple co-ordinate systems

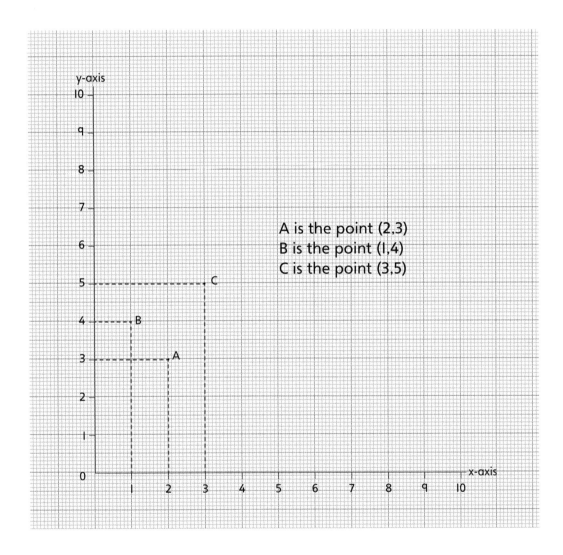

A is the point (2,3)
B is the point (1,4)
C is the point (3,5)

A Use graph paper. Draw an x-axis labelled from 0 to 10, and a y-axis labelled from 0 to 10, as shown in the illustration.
On the graph, plot these points.

A	(2,5)		B	(2,3)
C	(1,4)		D	(10,6)
E	(7,9)		F	(8,2)
G	(5,8)		H	(10,10)

More coordinates

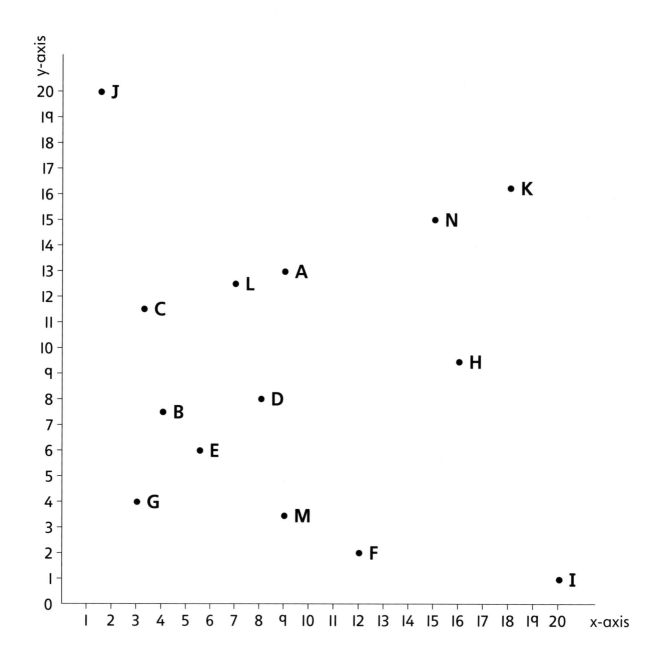

A Give the coordinates of each point on the graph above.

B Draw x- and y-axes and label each axis from 0 to 10. Now plot the following points and join them in the order written below.

(1,1), (1,8), (5,8), (5,7), (2,7), (2,6), (4,6), (4,5), (2,5), (2,1), (1,1)
Name the figure you have drawn.

Why do you need to use coordinates when you work with data? Think of some places you have used coordinates to help you find data.

Data collection

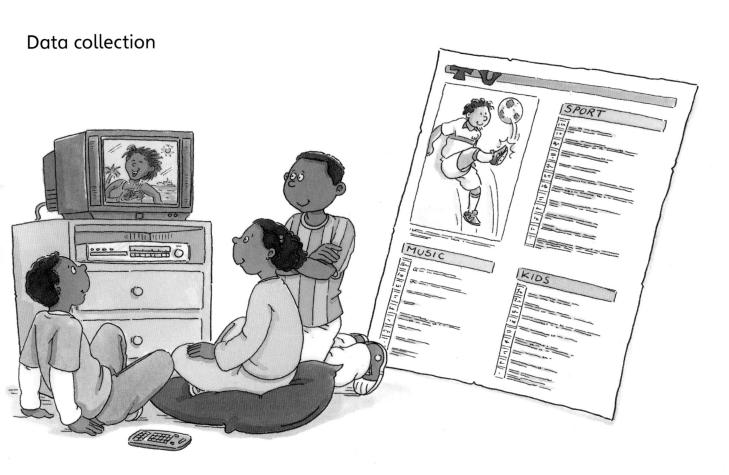

A **1** What is your favourite TV show?

2 a What do you think are the favourite TV shows of your classmates?

b How would you find out this information?

3 a Find out the favourite TV show of each student in your class.

b Make a list of all the shows they named and how many students named each show as their favourite. Write this information in the table like the one below.

Favourite TV show	Number of students

4 a What is the most popular show among your classmates?

b What is the least popular show among your classmates?

c What else can you deduce from the information you found?

Surveys

A On the right is a collection of items.

1 Explain which items would be useful for finding out the following:

a How many roads are in the main city in your territory?

b Whether the inhabitants of your town would like a new hotel to be built on the main road?

c How many cars stop at a particular set of traffic lights within 5 minutes?

2 Explain how each of the items can help people to gather information.

B How would you find out how many vehicles of each colour pass through your main town in an hour?

1 Go to one of the busiest areas in your main town. For one hour, observe the colours of the vehicles that pass by. Fill out a table like the one below. Use tallies to record each car that passes. After the hour, add up how many vehicles of each colour passed.

Colour of vehicle	Tally	Total
red	ЖЖ ЖЖ ЖЖ	15

2 **a** What was the most common colour?

b What was the least common colour?

c What was the difference in numbers between cars with the most common colour and the least common colour?

More surveys

A

1 The school needs to know which subjects are most popular among the students, and why.

a Name some ways in which the school could find out this information.
b Write down some of the questions you would ask to collect this information.
c Now interview all the students in your class and complete a table like the one below.

Subject	Number of students who prefer this subject

2 When you have completed your table, answer the following questions.

a Which is the most popular subject?
b Why is it the most popular?
c How many students like this subject most?
d Which is the least popular subject?
e Why do you think it is the least popular?
f What do you think could be done to make it more popular?

B
Carry out another survey to find out the most popular food, or the most popular music among students in your class. Select an appropriate way to represent your findings.

C
Your class is going on an outing, and the school canteen is preparing packed lunches. The cook in the canteen wants to find out who is going, and which sandwiches, cake, fruit and soft drinks are the most popular, so that she can use those in the packed lunches.

1 The canteen offers 4 types of sandwich, 3 types of cake, 5 different fruits and 3 kinds of soft drinks. Each pupil can choose any 2 sandwiches, and one of each of the other items.

a Decide which kinds of sandwich, cake, fruits and soft drinks you want to include in your survey. Make sure you provide the right number of choices for each item.
b Make a survey sheet that will collect the information that the cook needs.

2 a Carry out a survey of your class, using your survey sheet, to find out the most popular foods.
b Use the data you have collected to answer the cook's questions.
c Write what you discovered in your survey.
d If the cook puts the most popular foods and drinks in the packed lunches, what will each lunch include?

Collecting and representing data

Ways of representing data

Information is only useful when it is presented in a way that is easy to understand. For example, a long list of students' names and ages is not very easy to read; it would be easier to read the information from a bar graph showing how many students fall into each age group. Tally charts and pictographs can represent large numbers of people or items. Bar graphs can represent contrasting figures or amounts by representing each amount as a bar. Line graphs can represent changes, such as changes in temperature, population or prices.

Tables and tally charts

A This chart shows how many blank audio cassettes, DVDs and CDs of different lengths are in stock at Marty's Hi-Tek Electronics Store. Look at the chart and answer the questions.

	60 minute	90 minute	120 minute
CD	93	44	73
audio cassette	25	21	34
DVD	45	102	65

a How many 120-minute DVDs are in stock?
b How many 60-minute CDs are in stock?
c How many 90-minute audio cassettes are in stock?
d How many items are there altogether?
e How many more 90-minute items are in stock than 60-minute items?
f How many more CDs are there than audio cassettes and DVDs?
g How many more DVDs are there than audio cassettes?

B Look at the list of tally numbers.
a What number does I show?
b What number does ЖHt show?
c What number does ЖHt II show?
d What number does ЖHt ЖHt show?

Tally	Number
I	1
II	2
III	3
IIII	4
ЖHt	5
ЖHt I	6
ЖHt II	7
ЖHt III	8
ЖHt IIII	9
ЖHt ЖHt	10

C Look at the tally chart, and answer the questions.

	Class 3	Class 4
Girls	ЖHt ЖHt ЖHt IIII	ЖHt ЖHt ЖHt I
Boys	ЖHt ЖHt ЖHt III	ЖHt ЖHt ЖHt II

a How many boys are in Class 4?
b How many girls are in Class 3?
c How many more girls than boys are in Class 3?
d How many boys are there in Class 3 and Class 4 altogether?
e How many more boys than girls are there in Class 4?

Bar graphs

A A group of students was asked to name their favourite after-school activity. Each child had to choose one activity as their favourite. Look at the bar graph of favourite activities, then answer the questions.

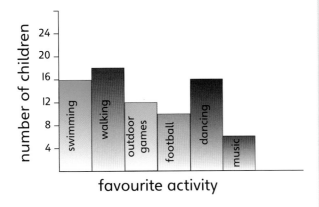

a How many children prefer swimming?
b How many children prefer football?
c How many children prefer walking?
d How many children prefer outdoor games?
e How many children prefer music?
f What is the most popular activity?
g What is the least popular activity?

B This bar graph shows how Pat spends her weekly wages.

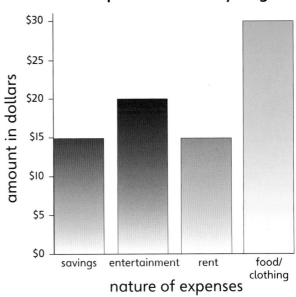

a How much does Pat save?
b How much rent does she pay?
c How much does she spend on food, clothing and entertainment altogether?
d What is Pat's weekly wage?
e How much would Pat earn in four weeks?

C This bar graph shows how a group of children travel to school. Use the graph to help you answer the questions.

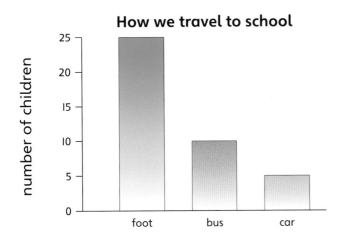

a How do most children travel to school?
b What is the least used type of transport shown?
c How many pupils travel by car and by bus altogether?
d What is the difference between the number of pupils who walk and the number who travel by car?

Collecting and representing data

Using bar graphs

Do a survey of your class to find out how most pupils travel to school. Use a tally chart to collect the information, and then draw a bar graph to present your findings. Use an appropriate scale on your graph making sure that it is clear to read.

B On Sports Day eight pupils made three jumps each. Their longest jumps were recorded in the graph. Use the graph to answer these questions.

a What was the longest jump and who made it?

b What was the shortest jump and who made it?

c Which pupils jumped further than 330 cm?

d How many pupils jumped further than Lucy?

e Who jumped further than Bob?

f How much further than Sue did Chris jump?

g Sara's shortest jump was 49 cm less than her longest jump. How far was her shortest jump?

h Todd's other two jumps were 306 cm and 321 cm. How much further than his shortest jump was his longest jump?

i What is the average of the longest jumps?

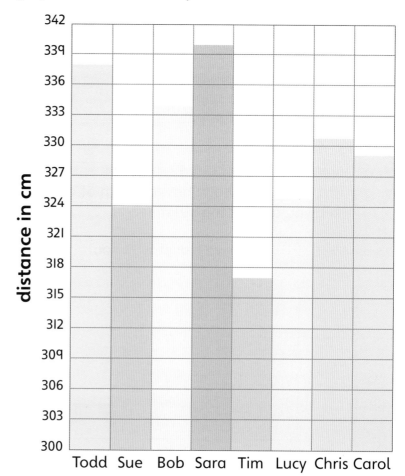

More bar graphs

A Copy and complete the bar graph using information from the table.

Month	Rainfall in cm
January	14
February	10
March	9
April	9
May	15
June	24

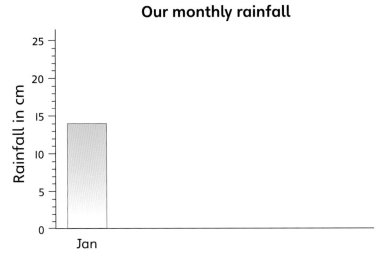

Our monthly rainfall

Now answer the questions.

a Which month had the highest rainfall?
b Which months had the same amount of rain?
c How much rain fell during the first three months?
d Which months had more rain than January?
e How much rain fell for the six months?
f What was the average rainfall for the six months?

B Copy and complete these tables, and then draw bar graphs to show the information.

a Favourite fruits

Fruits	Tallies	Number of children
mangoes	卌 卌 卌 I	
bananas	卌 III	
guavas	IIII	
pineapple	卌 IIII	

b Vehicles Tom saw one day

Vehicles	Tallies	Number of vehicles
cars	卌 卌 卌 IIII	
buses	卌 卌 IIII	
bicycles	卌 卌 卌 I	

c Favourite colours

Colours	Tallies	Number of children
red	卌 卌 I	
blue	卌 卌 卌	
green	卌 卌 卌 I	
yellow	卌 III	

d Types of car Jenny saw in an hour

Type	Tallies	Number of cars
Honda		
Ford	卌 I	
Mazda		
Nissan	卌 卌 卌 I	

Collecting and representing data

Making a graph about yourself

You will need: Graph paper, a ruler and a piece of string about I metre long.
What to do:

1. Ask a friend to measure your height in centimetres.

2. Measure your foot.

3. Use the string to measure the distance around your waist.

4. Use the string to measure the distance around your neck.

5. Record your measurements in a table like the one below.

6. Make a graph to show the information in your table. Let each large square on the graph paper represent 10 cm.

	Measurement in cm
Height	
Foot	
Waist	
Neck	

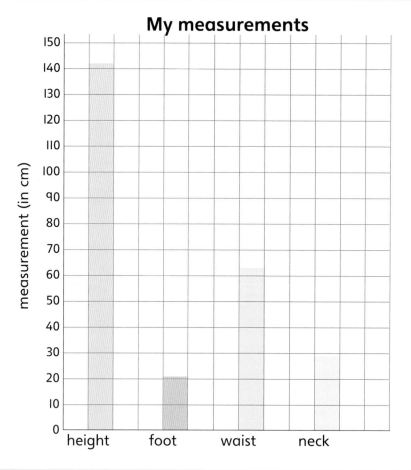

In which jobs do you need to spend a lot of time measuring things in centimetres and millimetres? What kind of measuring instruments or equipment would you need for these jobs?

Collecting and representing data

Problem solving with graphs

A There were 20 students in a class. They received these scores in a mathematics test.

1. Copy and complete a table like this one to show how many students received each score.

Scores	Tallies	Number of students
1		
2		
3		
4		
5		

2. Use graph paper. Draw a bar graph to represent the information in the table.

3.
   a. What percentage of the students received scores of 6?
   b. What percentage of the class received scores above 6?
   c. What was the average score?
   d. Find the sum of the percentages in a, b and c.

B *You will need:* A newspaper cutting like the one showing football results telling you how many goals were scored by each team.

Arsenal	1	Manchester City	2
Crystal Palace	1	Nottingham Forest	2
Leeds United	0	Aston Villa	1
Liverpool	3	Tottenham Hotspur	0

1. Make a table to show the number of teams who scored 0, 1, 2, 3 goals.

2. Draw a graph of your results. Label the x-axis 'number of goals', and the y-axis 'frequency'. For example, if 7 teams each scored 5 goals, the bar labelled 5 goals would extend to the frequency of 7. Don't forget to use a suitable scale for your axes.

Goals scored	Tally marks	Number of teams
0	||	
1	|||	
2	||	
3	|	

3.
   a. How many goals were scored most frequently?
   b. How many goals were scored the least frequently?

Collecting and representing data

Tally charts and pictographs

A **1** Copy and complete this tally chart.

Games	Tallies	Number of children
cricket	卌 卌 IIII	
tennis	卌 III	
basketball	卌 IIII	
football	卌 卌 II	

2 Peter started this pictograph to show the information from the tally chart above.

a How many children does one circle represent?

b Copy and complete Peter's pictograph.

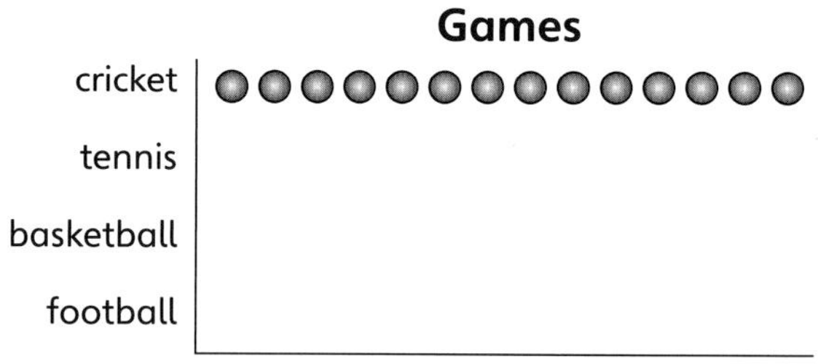

Games

cricket ⊙⊙⊙⊙⊙⊙⊙⊙⊙⊙⊙⊙⊙⊙
tennis
basketball
football

3 a Copy and complete this tally chart.

Favourite ice cream	Tallies	Number of children
Vanilla	卌 卌	
Chocolate	IIII	
Strawberry	卌 卌 I	
Pineapple	卌 III	

b Using the information from question a, work out how many children 👤 represents in this pictograph.

c How many children does 👤 represent?

Favourite ice cream

vanilla

chocolate

strawberry

pineapple

B Yasmin did a survey of the students in her class to see how many have had various illnesses.

Illness	Tally	Frequency
rubella	卌 卌 卌	
chickenpox	卌 卌 IIII	14
flu	卌 卌 卌 卌 I	
measles	卌 卌 III	
whooping cough	卌	
mumps	卌 I	

a List the illnesses.

b Write down how many pupils have had each illness.

Collecting and representing data

Pictographs

Ice-cream cones sold

represents 8 ice-cream cones

1. a Make a tally chart to show how many cones were sold each day.
   b On which day were most cones sold?
   c Why do you think the most cones were sold on that day?

2. a If represents 150 men, how many men does represent?
   b If represents 300 bananas, how many does show?

3. ● represents 400 oranges.
   a How many oranges does ●●●● represent?
   b How many oranges does ●●●●◖ represent?
   c Draw how you would represent 2 200 oranges.

4. represents 100 sweets.
   How many sweets are represented in the following:
   a   b

B Harry is a fisherman. His weekly catch is shown in the table below. Draw a pictograph, using fish, to show this information. Remember to write how many kilograms one picture of a fish represents.

Weight of weekly catch

Week	Kilograms of fish
1st	40
2nd	30
3rd	50
4th	10
5th	30

More pictographs

In the pictograph 👧 stands for 4 pupils.

class 1	👧👧👧👧👧👧👧👧
class 2	👧👧👧👧👧👧👧
class 3	👧👧👧👧👧

1
  a What does 👧 stand for?
  b How many pupils are there in each class?

2 From the information in this table, draw a pictograph to show the number of houses in four streets. Use 🏠 to represent 10 houses.

Street	Number of houses
Crab Street	40
High Street	35
Old Avenue	60
Cross Road	55

B

Letters collected from postbox

Monday	✉✉✉✉✉✉✉✉
Tuesday	✉✉✉✉✉
Wednesday	✉✉✉✉
Thursday	✉✉✉✉✉✉✉
Friday	✉✉✉✉✉✉
Saturday	✉✉✉

This pictograph shows the number of letters collected from a postbox during one week.

a On which day did the postman collect the most letters?
b On which day did the postman collect the fewest letters?
c On which day did the postman collect twice as many letters as he did on Wednesday?
d On which day did the postman collect half as many letters as he did on Friday?
e Did you need to know how many letters the symbol ✉ represents to answer questions a to d? Try to give a reason for your answer.
f If ✉ represents 12 letters, how many more letters were collected on Monday than were collected on Saturday?

Line graphs

A This line graph shows the temperatures in Trinidad at 12 noon over a period of 2 weeks.

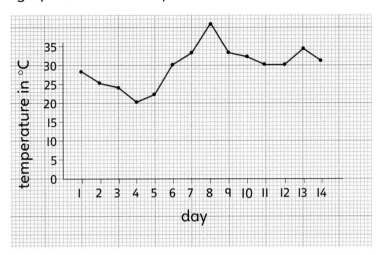

1 a Which day had the highest temperature at noon?
b Which day had the lowest temperature?
c What were these temperatures?

2 During which season do you think this graph was drawn?

3 a Between which two consecutive days was there the greatest drop in temperature? What was the difference in temperature between these two days?
b Between which two consecutive days was there the greatest rise in temperature?
c What was the difference in temperature between these two days?

4 Using a thermometer, record the temperature in your classroom for a week. Draw a graph to show your findings.

B The line graph below shows the population of the world over 250 years.

1 a When did the population start to grow at a much faster rate than before?
b How do you know?

2 a When did the world population reach 1 billion?
b After it had reached 1 billion, how many years did it take for the population to double?
c When did the world population reach 6 billion?

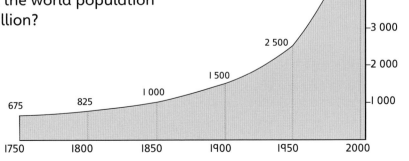

Collecting and representing data

Averages

Which number occurs most often? This is the mode.

> The mode of a set of numbers is the number that occurs the most often. For example:
> In the set: 5, 8, 2, 3, 2, 2
> The mode is 2.
> A set may have more than one mode. For example:
> In the set: 4, 5, 5, 6, 8, 8, 9
> The modes are 5 and 8.

A In a gymnastics competition, these were the scores for each competitor.

1   **a**   Find the mode for each competitor's scores.
         b   Find the overall mode.

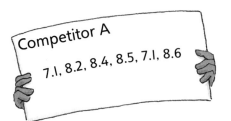

Competitor A

7.1, 8.2, 8.4, 8.5, 7.1, 8.6

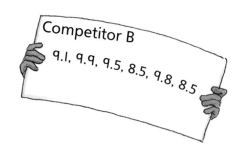

Competitor B

9.1, 9.9, 9.5, 8.5, 9.8, 8.5

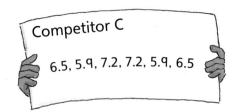

Competitor C

6.5, 5.9, 7.2, 7.2, 5.9, 6.5

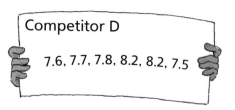

Competitor D

7.6, 7.7, 7.8, 8.2, 8.2, 7.5

2   Do you think the competitors should receive their official score from the average or from the mode of their six scores? Explain your answer.

B For each of the following sets, find the mode.

   a   89, 95, 99, 99, 190, 199, 200   **b**   165, 120, 121, 159, 120, 121

   c   6, 6, 6, 7, 7, 8, 8, 9, 9, 9, 10, 11, 11, 11, 11   **d**   45, 56, 65, 65, 76, 78

   e   1.1, 1.2, 1.1, 1.1, 1.3, 1.3, 1.5, 1.3, 1.2, 1.6, 1.2, 1.5, 1.2

Modes

A A group of students were practising getting the basketball into the basket. Each student had 10 tries. This is how many baskets they made.

Name	Baskets
Jenny	ЦИТ
David	ЦИТ II
Michelle	II
Dinah	III
Gareth	
Sue	ЦИТ III
Benjamin	ЦИТ ЦИТ
Harry	IIII
Joe	III
Mike	ЦИТ II
Lisa	ЦИТ I
Billy	ЦИТ II
Tina	ЦИТ III
Amal	ЦИТ ЦИТ
Linda	IIII
Dan	ЦИТ IIII
Gary	ЦИТ IIII
Wayne	ЦИТ III
Andrew	ЦИТ I
Liz	ЦИТ III

1 What was the mode of their scores?

2 a Go outside and practise getting a ball through a basket or hoop. Another way to play this game is to practise throwing a coin into an empty tin. Each student should get 10 chances.
   b Make tally charts to record each student's score.
   c Find the mode of your scores.
   d Draw a bar chart to show the scores.

B 1 a Find out the ages of everyone in your class.
        b Work out the mode of your classmate's ages.
     2 a Find out how many brothers and sisters your classmates have.
        b Work out the mode.
     3 a Ask 30 different people what month they were born in. Draw a bar graph showing your findings.
        b Work out the mode.

Collecting and representing data

The mean

Consider the following numbers:
5, 1, 9, 8, 3, 4

$$\text{Mean} = \frac{5+1+9+8+3+4}{6}$$
$$= \frac{30}{6}$$
$$= 5$$

You have already done this in an earlier chapter. Can you remember the other name for mean?

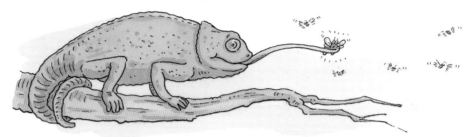

A **1** The table below shows how many flies the chameleon ate every day for a week.

Monday	Tuesday	Wednesday	Thursday	Friday	Saturday	Sunday
7	2	4	6	1	4	3

   a   Find the mode for the week.
   b   Find the mean number of flies.
   c   Draw a line graph showing the consumption of flies over the week.

2 Find the mean amount of drink left in each set of glasses.
   a   100 ml, 110 ml, 90 ml, 75 ml, 122 ml, 137 ml

   b   233 ml, 210 ml, 198 ml, 188 ml, 240 ml, 190 ml

   c   35 ml, 15 ml, 28 ml, 18 ml, 29 ml, 34 ml

   d   142 ml, 164 ml, 133 ml, 182 ml, 152 ml, 160 ml

3 Identify the pattern in each set, and then find the mean of the set.
   a   16, 14, 12, 10, 8   b   1, 2, 3, 5, 7, 11, 13
   c   1, 4, 9, 16, 25, 36   d   66, 55, 44, 33, 22, 11
   e   1, 2, 4, 7, 11, 16, 21

More about the mean

A **1** The table shows the mass of six children.
- **a** Find the mean mass of the boys.
- **b** Find the mean mass of the girls.
- **c** Find the mean mass of the children.

Name	Weight in kg
Peter	38.2
Pam	35
John	35.4
Charles	38.4
Maureen	33.48
Desmond	42

2 This table shows the amount Michael saved each month from May to August one year.
Find the mean of his monthly savings.

Month	Amount saved
May	$ 17.25
June	$ 18.50
July	$ 15.65
August	$ 13.20

3 This table shows the amount saved by five of a group of six children.
- **a** What was the mean amount saved by the girls?
- **b** If the boys had the same mean as the girls, how much did John save?

Name	Amount saved
Mary	$ 16.50
Sue	$ 18.45
Peter	$ 20.16
John	____
Vincent	$ 15.84
Sharon	$ 21.48

4

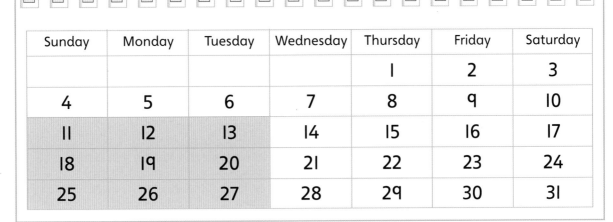

Sunday	Monday	Tuesday	Wednesday	Thursday	Friday	Saturday
				1	2	3
4	5	6	7	8	9	10
11	12	13	14	15	16	17
18	19	20	21	22	23	24
25	26	27	28	29	30	31

- **a** Find the mean of the numbers inside the box marked on the calendar.
- **b** Mark off another three-by-three box of numbers on your copy of the calendar. Find the mean of the numbers you have boxed.
- **c** Look at the two means you have worked out. Is there a pattern?
- **d** What will be the mean for any three-by-three box of numbers on the calendar?

Collecting and representing data

Assessment

A Jimmy has a stand on the beach selling T-shirts. He keeps a tally of how many T-shirts he sells each day.

Kind of T-shirt	Monday	Tuesday	Wednesday	Thursday	Friday	Saturday	Sunday
plain red			|	||	||		||
surfer	|		||	|	||||	ЖHT	ЖHT ||||
shells	||		ЖHT		ЖHT	|||	|
plain blue	|			||	|||		|||
starfish	ЖHT |		|||	|	ЖHT ||||	ЖHT ЖHT	ЖHT ЖHT ЖHT ||

\| = 1 T-shirt

ЖHT = 5 T-shirts

1
  a How many T-shirts did he sell altogether?
  b What kind of T-shirts were the most popular?
  c On which day did he make the lowest sales?

2 Draw a pictograph showing Jimmy's sales of each kind of T-shirt.

3 Draw a bar graph showing Jimmy's sales each day of the week.

4
  a Calculate the average number of T-shirts sold from Friday to Sunday.
  b Calculate the average number of T-shirts sold between Monday and Friday.

5 Explain how you would use this information if you were Jimmy.

B **1** Collect three different kinds of graphs or charts from newspapers or magazines. For each piece of data, explain how the information has been represented, and why you think the researcher has chosen this way to represent the data.